Presented To

By

Occasion

Date

Deep Blue Bible Storybook

No part of this work may be reproduced or transmitted in any form or by any means, electronic or mechanical, including photocopying and recording, or by any information storage or retrieval system, except as may be expressly permitted by the 1976 Copyright Act or by permission in writing from the publisher. Requests for permission should be submitted in writing to: Rights and Permissions, The United Methodist Publishing House, 2222 Rosa L. Parks Blvd., Nashville, TN 37228-1306; faxed to 615-749-6128; or submitted via e-mail to *permissions@abingdonpress.com*.

Scripture quotations are taken from the Common English Bible, copyright © 2011. Used by permission. All rights reserved.

Co-written by Kerry Blackwood, Daphna Flegal, and Brittany Sky; with special thanks to Elizabeth F. Caldwell
Editor: Brittany Sky
Designer: Matthew Allison

Cover Art (Deep Blue Kids) by: Tim Moen (Character Design), Jesse Griffin (3D Artist), Julio Medina (3D Artist), Eric M. Mikula (Facial Rigging), and Christopher Slavik (Layout Artist); background: Four Story Creative.

Art: Four Story Creative; Deep Blue Kids illustrations by Tim Moen, Jesse Griffin, Julio Medina, Eric M. Mikula, and Christopher Slavik.

ISBN: 9781501848612

20 21 22 23 24 25 26 27 28 29—10 9 8 7 6 5 4 3 2 1

Printed in China

To the Grownups

One of the first songs that children learn in church is "Jesus Loves Me." In this first musical affirmation of faith, they confess that they know that Jesus loves them because the Bible tells them this through stories written across time and cultures. In singing this song and in reading stories about Jesus, a child's spiritual formation begins. But if a child's faith is going to continue to grow with that child, then something more is needed.

Children participate in church educational programs and learn many Bible stories. They possess a lot of factual knowledge about Miriam and Moses, Abraham and Sarah, Ruth and Naomi, David, the stories of Jesus and the people he met, and the beginnings of the church which are told in Acts and the Epistles. Such learning is an important building block in their spiritual formation, and teachers are very important spiritual guides for our children.

But nothing is more important than providing time with a Bible storybook—like this one—engaging children's curiosities about the Bible. Equally essential is the chance for them to ask their own questions about biblical texts, to wonder about the story, to reflect on how they understand and interpret it, and the meaning it has for their lives. This chance for children to engage the Bible with all their curiosity and questions contributes to their development of a language of faith. A child's spiritual formation is as important as her or his growth in the child's abilities as a student, an athlete, a musician, or an artist. And this spiritual formation is incomplete if it only happens in the church. As good as such ministries are, they are insufficient unless supported by parents and families at home.

Children have very important questions about the biblical texts, about the variety of faith expressions they experience in congregations, and about the comments other children make to them, as well as the ones they overhear from adults. As you read Bible stories with children, encourage their questions—the ways they wrestle with the stories they hear. Don't be afraid of questions they ask! Encourage them and join them in this wonderful experience of reading the Bible together. In this way, they won't grow out of it, but rather each time they visit a story, new questions will emerge. It is an incredible spiritual practice that will grow with a child and with you!

Blessings,
Elizabeth Caldwell
author of *I Wonder: Engaging a Child's Curiosity about the Bible*

To the Children From the Deep Blue Kids

Hi, friends! We're glad you are here to dive deep with us into God's Word. We'll have adventures and learn fun facts on our journey.

The Bible is more than just a big book; it's a gift to us from God! It's also a gift to us from many people. It took hundreds of years and thousands of people to bring us this gift. And like all good gifts, the Bible is meant to be opened, explored, and enjoyed. It's our hope that you will learn more about God, the Bible, Jesus, faith, and how it all fits into life today.

Contents

Genesis   1

The Earth	(Genesis 1:1-19)	2
Living Things	(Genesis 1:20-25)	6
In God's Image	(Genesis 1:26–2:4)	9
Adam and Eve	(Genesis 2:10–3:24)	12
Noah Builds the Ark	(Genesis 6:13-22)	16
Two of Every Kind	(Genesis 7:1-16)	18
Sending Out the Dove	(Genesis 8:1-19)	20
The Rainbow Promise	(Genesis 8:20–9:17)	23
Abraham and Sarah	(Genesis 12:1-9; 15:1-6)	26
Abraham and Lot	(Genesis 13:1-12)	28
The Birth of Isaac	(Genesis 18:1-15; 21:1-7)	32
Isaac and Rebekah	(Genesis 24:1-67)	35
Jacob and Esau	(Genesis 25:19-28)	38
The Birthright	(Genesis 25:29-34)	40
The Blessing	(Genesis 27:1-46)	42
Jacob's Ladder	(Genesis 28:10-22)	45
Joseph and His Brothers	(Genesis 37:1-36)	46
Joseph in Egypt	(Genesis 39:1–40:23)	48
Joseph Saves the Day	(Genesis 41:1-57)	52
Joseph and His Brothers Reunited	(Genesis 42:1–46:34)	55

Exodus   59

The Baby in the Basket	(Exodus 1:8-14; 2:1-10)	60
The Burning Bush	(Exodus 2:11–3:22)	64
Moses and Pharaoh	(Exodus 5:1–13:9)	68
Crossing the Sea	(Exodus 13:17–14:31)	71
Songs of Joy	(Exodus 15:1-21)	74
In the Wilderness	(Exodus 15:22–17:7)	76
Ten Commandments	(Exodus 19:1–20:21)	80
A House for God	(Exodus 25–31:15; 35:4–40:38)	84

Joshua   87
God Chooses Joshua   (Joshua 1:1-9)   88
Spies in Canaan   (Joshua 2:1-24)   92
Crossing the Jordan   (Joshua 3:1-17; 4:1-24)   97
Jericho   (Joshua 6:1-27)   100

Ruth   103
Goodness   (Book of Ruth)   104

1 Samuel   109
Hannah Prays   (1 Samuel 1:1-28)   110
God Calls Samuel   (1 Samuel 3:1-21)   114
Samuel Anoints Saul   (1 Samuel 7:15–8:22; 10:17-24)   118
Samuel Anoints David   (1 Samuel 16:1-23)   122
David the Musician   (1 Samuel 16:14-23)   125
David and Goliath   (1 Samuel 17:1-51a)   129
David and Jonathan   (1 Samuel 18:1-5; 20:1-42)   134
David and Abigail   (1 Samuel 25:1-42)   138

2 Samuel   141
David Dances   (2 Samuel 6:1-19)   142
Kindness   (2 Samuel 9:1-13)   145

1 Kings   149
Solomon Becomes King   (1 Kings 2:1-4; 3:1-15)   150
Solomon Builds
the Temple   (1 Kings 6:1-38)   152
Solomon Dedicates
the Temple   (1 Kings 8:1-66)   155
Elijah and the Ravens   (1 Kings 16:29-30; 17:1-7)   158
Elijah and the Prophets   (1 Kings 18:20-39)   160

2 Kings   163
Faithfulness   (2 Kings 22:1–23:23)   164

Contents

Elisha and the Widow's Jars	(2 Kings 4:1-7)	168
Elisha and the Servant Girl	(2 Kings 5:1-19)	172

Esther — 177
Courageous Queen	(Book of Esther)	178

Psalms — 183
Gentleness	(Psalm 23:1-6)	184
Joy	(Psalm 100:1-5)	186

Proverbs — 187
Solomon's Wisdom
Proverbs	(Proverbs 6:6-8; 10:1; 17:17)	188

Isaiah — 191
The Peaceable Kingdom	(Isaiah 11:6-9)	192

Jeremiah — 193
A Baby Is Coming	(Jeremiah 23:5-8)	194

Daniel — 195
Self-control	(Daniel 1:1-21)	196
Courageous Friends	(Daniel 3:1-30)	200
Courageous Daniel	(Daniel 6:1-28)	204

Jonah — 209
Jonah and the Fish	(Book of Jonah)	210

Matthew — 215
Joseph's Story	(Matthew 1:18-24)	216
Follow the Star	(Matthew 2:1-12)	218
Come to the River	(Matthew 3:13-17)	221
Jesus Calls the Fishermen	(Matthew 4:18-22)	223
Peace	(Matthew 5:1-9)	226
The Lord's Prayer	(Matthew 6:5-15)	228
The Birds of the Air	(Matthew 6:25-34)	230

The Golden Rule | (Matthew 7:12) | 233
The Two Houses | (Matthew 7:24-27) | 234
The Man in the Synagogue | (Matthew 12:9-14) | 236
Jesus and the Children | (Matthew 19:13-15) | 239
Hosanna! | (Matthew 21:1-11) | 242
At the Last Supper | (Matthew 26:17-30) | 246
In the Garden | (Matthew 26:31-58) | 250
Cock-a-doodle-doo! | (Matthew 26:69-75) | 256
Alleluia! | (Matthew 28:1-10) | 260
The Great Commission | (Matthew 28:16-20) | 263

Mark — 265

A Voice in the Wilderness | (Mark 1:9-11) | 266
The Four Friends | (Mark 2:1-12) | 268
Jesus Calms the Storm | (Mark 4:35-41) | 272
Jairus's Daughter | (Mark 5:21-24, 35-43) | 276
Go Two by Two | (Mark 6:7-13) | 280
Bartimaeus Shouts to Jesus | (Mark 10:46-52) | 282
People Welcome Jesus | (Mark 11:1-11) | 285
Jesus Breaks the Bread | (Mark 14:12-26) | 288

Luke — 293

Elizabeth and Zechariah | (Luke 1:5-25) | 294
Gabriel's Message | (Luke 1:26-38) | 298
Mary Visits Elizabeth | (Luke 1:39-66) | 302
Jesus Is Born | (Luke 2:1-7) | 304
Joyous News | (Luke 2:8-20) | 308
Simeon and Anna | (Luke 2:25-31) | 310
Talk With the Teachers | (Luke 2:39-52) | 313
Jesus Is Baptized | (Luke 3:1-22) | 317
Jesus Chooses | (Luke 4:1-13) | 320
Jesus Brings Good News | (Luke 4:14-30) | 323

Contents

Jesus Heals	(Luke 4:38-44)	326
Jesus Calls Levi	(Luke 5:27-32)	329
The Two Debtors	(Luke 7:41-43)	332
Women Follow Jesus	(Luke 8:1-3)	334
The Sower	(Luke 8:4-15)	336
The Good Samaritan	(Luke 10:25-37)	340
Mary and Martha	(Luke 10:38-42)	347
The Mustard Seed & the Yeast	(Luke 13:18-21)	350
The Stories of the Lost	(Luke 15:3-10)	352
The Forgiving Father	(Luke 15:11-32)	356
Ten Lepers	(Luke 17:11-19)	362
Patience	(Luke 18:1-8)	366
The Pharisee & the Tax Collector	(Luke 18:9-14)	368
Zacchaeus	(Luke 19:1-10)	372
The Ten Talents	(Luke 19:11-26)	376
Jesus Enters Jerusalem	(Luke 19:28-40)	379
The Widow's Coins	(Luke 21:1-4)	382
Jesus Celebrates Passover	(Luke 22:7-20)	384
The Tomb Is Empty	(Luke 24:1-12)	388
The Road to Emmaus	(Luke 24:13-35)	392
John		**395**
Change the Water	(John 2:1-12)	396
Born Anew	(John 3:1-21)	400
The Woman at the Well	(John 4:1-42)	404
The Man by the Pool	(John 5:1-17)	408
A Boy's Lunch	(John 6:1-15)	412
Jesus Walks on Water	(John 6:16-25)	418
Mary Honors Jesus	(John 12:1-8)	424
Jesus Washes Feet	(John 13:1-17)	428
Jesus Lives	(John 20:1-18)	431

Thomas Believes	(John 20:24-31)	435
Come to Breakfast!	(John 21:1-14)	438
Feed My Sheep!	(John 21:15-19)	442

Acts 445

Pentecost	(Acts 2:1-41)	446
Peter and John	(Acts 3:1–4:22)	450
Believers Share	(Acts 4:32-37)	453
Choosing the Seven	(Acts 6:1-7)	455
Philip and the Ethiopian	(Acts 8:26-40)	458
Paul Changes	(Acts 9:1-19)	462
Paul Escapes	(Acts 9:20-25)	466
The Church Grows	(Acts 9:26-31)	469
Peter and Tabitha	(Acts 9:36-43)	471
Peter and Cornelius	(Acts 10:1-28)	475
First Called Christians	(Acts 11:19-30)	481
Peter in Prison	(Acts 12:1-17)	484
Timothy Is Chosen	(Acts 16:1-5)	489
Lydia	(Acts 16:11-15)	490
Paul and Silas	(Acts 16:16-40)	492
Shipwrecked	(Acts 27:1-44)	496

1 Corinthians 501

We Are One Body	(1 Corinthians 12:12-31)	502
Love	(1 Corinthians 13:1-13)	505

Prayers & Songs 507

How God Wants Us to Live	508
Nativity Songs	511
Easter and Blessings Songs	513
Mealtime Prayers	515
Movement Prayer	516

Genesis

Did you know *genesis* means "beginning"? The Book of Genesis tells the stories of Creation and the stories of the beginning of God's people!

Tips for **Adults**

The authors of Genesis sought to answer the question, "Where did we come from?" The Book of Genesis tells us about the amazing beginning of the world. God created the earth, sky, and everything in the world. God made human beings to enjoy and to take care of the world. This book also explains the beginning of God's people, the Israelites.

2

The Earth
Genesis 1:1-19

In the beginning, there was nothing. The earth was empty and shapeless. God spoke, "Let there be light," and light was made. God separated light from dark. God called light Day and dark Night.

When reading the book, chapter, and verse, say, "The Book of Genesis, chapter 1, verses 1 through 19," so the children learn about how the Bible is organized.

Then God said, "Let there be sky," and there was a sky. Then God said, "Let there be water and dry land." God called the dry land Earth and the waters Seas.

Then God said, "Let there be plants on the earth," and plants began growing on the earth.

Then God said, "Let there be a sun in the day sky, and a moon and stars in the night sky."

**God created all we see!
Where is your favorite place to
go in the earth God made?**

Living Things
Genesis 1:20-25

Then God said, "Let there be sea animals in the seas." The sea animals swam in the seas.

Then God said, "Let there be birds in the air." The birds flew in the air.

What is your favorite animal?

Then God said, "Let there be lots of animals all over the earth," and there were many kinds of animals living on the earth. God saw all that had been made and called it all good.

In God's Image
Genesis 1:26–2:4

God looked out on all that had been made and saw that it was all good, but something was missing.

God spoke, "Let there be people," and people were created. God saw the people and thought they were very good.

"The people will take care of my creation. They will look out for day and night; the sky, the seas, the earth; all of the plants, all of the sea animals and birds of the air, and all of the animals that live on the earth." God saw all that had been made and thought it was all supremely good.

How do you think God felt in this story?

Adam and Eve
Genesis 2:10–3:24

God made the first human to live in the garden of Eden. God asked the human to follow some rules, "Take care of this land. Eat from any tree in the garden, but you can't eat from the Tree of Good and Evil."

God noticed that the human was lonely in the garden. God said, "It's not good for the human to be alone. I will make a partner for him." God made all of the wild animals and all of the birds, and brought them to the human to name. The human named all of the animals, but none of the animals were a perfect fit for the human.

So God put the human to sleep. Then God made a woman. The human was excited and said, "This one is the perfect partner! She will be called a woman."

In the garden of Eden there lived a terrible snake. The snake told the woman, "Eat some fruit from the Tree of Good and Evil." She said, "No, Snake. God said, 'Do not eat that special fruit.'" But the snake talked her into eating the special fruit. The woman took a bite and gave some to the man. When God found out they had eaten the fruit, God said, "Look at what you have done! Now that you both have eaten my special fruit, life will be harder than it has been." Then God made Adam and Eve leave the garden of Eden.

? How do you think Adam and Eve felt in this story?
What could have been different in the story?

Noah Builds the Ark
Genesis 6:13-22

God told Noah that the world would be flooded and told Noah to build a wooden ark. God told Noah how to make the ark.

Noah would need to include places for animals to live and sleep. Noah was also going to need to cover it with tar inside and out.

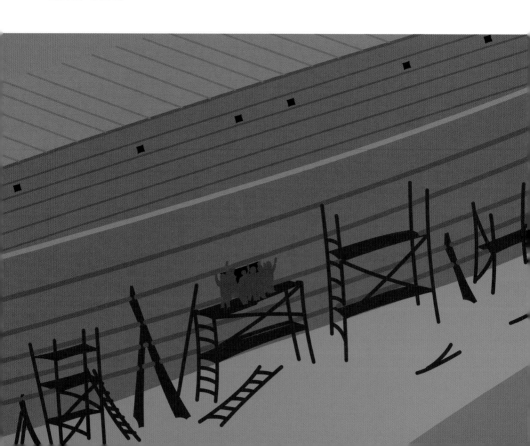

God told Noah he would need to bring his wife, his sons, and his sons' wives into the ark. God told Noah he would also need to bring two of every kind of bird, livestock, and crawling creature into the boat. Noah was told he would need to bring all kinds of food onto the ark. Noah did everything God told him to do.

What do you think Noah thought when God asked him to build a giant boat?

Two of Every Kind
Genesis 7:1-16

God told Noah it was time to load up the ark. Noah took his whole family into the ark with all of the different animals. God told Noah to take at least two of every kind of animal into the ark. Noah did everything God told him to do.

What do you think the animals were thinking while they were stuck inside?

When everyone had entered the ark—Noah and his family, and all of the creatures—the rain began to fall. It rained and rained.

Sending Out the Dove
Genesis 8:1-19

God did not forget Noah and the animals. God sent a wind over the earth, and the water dried up. The ark came to rest on a mountain.

Noah opened a window and sent out a raven. The raven flew back and forth until the waters had dried up over the land.

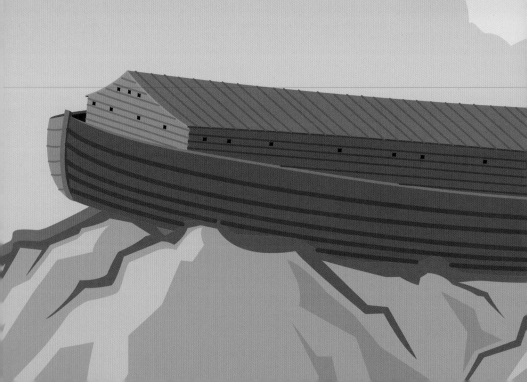

Then Noah sent out a dove to see if the waters on the fertile land had dried up, but the dove found no place to rest and returned to the ark.

Seven days later, Noah sent the dove out again. This time the dove returned in the evening with an olive leaf in its beak.

Seven days later, Noah sent the dove out again and it did not return. Noah knew that meant the water had dried up. It was time to open the door of the ark. All of the animals and all of the people came out of the ark onto the dry land.

How do you think everyone felt being back on dry land?

The Rainbow Promise
Genesis 8:20–9:17

Then Noah and his family praised and thanked God.

God thought, *I promise to never hurt the earth.* God blessed Noah and all of the creatures.

God made a promise to never again destroy all of the creatures. God placed a rainbow in the clouds. Whenever God and Noah see the rainbow, they will remember God's promise.

What's your favorite color in the rainbow?

Abraham and Sarah
Genesis 12:1-9; 15:1-6

God loved Abraham, and Abraham loved God. God said to Abraham, "Go where I send you, and I will bless you."

Abraham did what God told him to do. Abraham took his wife, Sarah, and his nephew, Lot. They packed up all of their things and went where God led them to go.

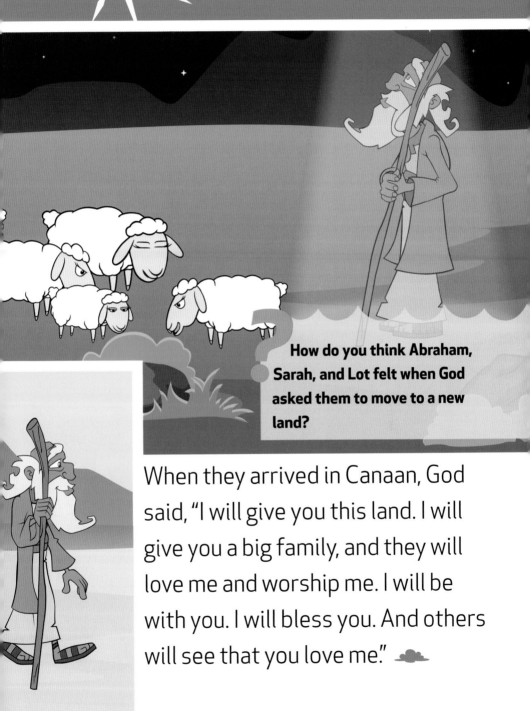

How do you think Abraham, Sarah, and Lot felt when God asked them to move to a new land?

When they arrived in Canaan, God said, "I will give you this land. I will give you a big family, and they will love me and worship me. I will be with you. I will bless you. And others will see that you love me."

Abraham and Lot
Genesis 13:1-12

Abraham had lots of cattle, sheep, goats, silver, and gold. Abraham moved from place to place so his animals could eat new grass. Abraham's nephew, Lot, also owned many sheep, goats, and cattle.

Lot and Abraham had shepherds who took care of their animals. One day the shepherds started fighting because there was not enough grass for all their animals to eat. Lot and Abraham had a problem!

Abraham said, "Let's not fight about this. Lot, look around at all the land. Choose a place to live. Then I will move in the other direction."

Lot looked around and said, "I really like the Jordan River Valley. It's pretty and green, and has good grass and plenty of water for my animals."

Abraham said, "Then you should move to the Jordan River Valley."

Abraham went to live in the Hebron Valley. God said to Abraham, "I will give you land as far as your eyes can see, and I will also bless you with a very large family."

How do you feel when you share?

The Birth of Isaac
Genesis 18:1-15; 21:1-7

One hot summer afternoon, Abraham was sitting outside his tent when three men walked up to him. Abraham welcomed the men. The guests sat down, while Abraham told Sarah to make a meal for the guests.

While the three men ate the meal, they asked Abraham, "Where is your wife, Sarah?"

Abraham said, "Sarah is in the tent."

One of the visitors said, "I will come back next year, and Sarah will have a new baby."

Sarah heard the visitor, and she laughed because she thought she was too old to have a baby.

The visitor said, "I do not know why you laugh, Sarah, because nothing is too hard for God to do."

The next year, Sarah did have a baby. Sarah and Abraham named their baby, Isaac. Sarah was full of joy because she had a new baby boy, and Sarah said, "Who would have thought that I would have a baby when I was 90 years old!"

Sarah and Abraham were joyful because they became parents to Isaac. What brings you joy?

Isaac and Rebekah
Genesis 24:1-67

Isaac grew from a baby to a man. Now it was time for Isaac to marry. Abraham called his servant, "Go to my family's home and find a wife for my son, Isaac." So the servant took ten camels and traveled to the city where Abraham's family lived.

The servant and all the camels stopped at the well just outside the city. Then the servant asked God for help. "Oh, God," the servant prayed, "show me the woman you want Isaac to marry."

The servant waited at the well. Soon, a young woman named Rebekah came by. She filled her water jar with water from the well.

"May I have a drink of your water?" asked the servant.

"Of course," answered Rebekah. "I'll get some water for your camels too."

This is the woman God wants Isaac to marry, thought the servant, so he went to meet Rebekah's family.

"God has chosen Rebekah as the wife for Abraham's son, Isaac," the servant said to Rebekah's family. "Will you let me take her home to marry Isaac?"

"Yes," answered Rebekah's family.

Isaac was waiting for them. Isaac and Rebekah were married.

The servant prayed to God for help when he had to make a choice. Who do you ask for help?

Jacob and Esau
Genesis 25:19-28

Isaac and Rebekah were getting older, and they wanted to have a family. They prayed to God for a baby. Rebekah became pregnant with twin boys! Their names were Esau and Jacob. They were born on the same day, but they were very different. Esau was born first. He had red hair on his head and arms. Jacob was born second. He had dark hair. Jacob and Esau liked different things. Esau liked to be outdoors. He liked to hunt, fish, and watch the animals play. Esau enjoyed spending time with Isaac. Jacob liked being inside the tent where his family was. He liked to cook, and made a delicious lentil stew. Jacob enjoyed spending time with Rebekah.

Esau liked to be outside and play outdoors. Jacob liked to be at home and to make food. What things do you like to do?

The Birthright
Genesis 25:29-34

One day Esau returned home from hunting. Jacob was making lentil stew, and Esau was very hungry.

"Can I have some lentil stew and some bread, please, Jacob?" Esau asked.

Would you have made the same choice as Esau?

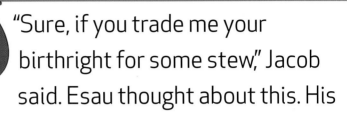

"Sure, if you trade me your birthright for some stew," Jacob said. Esau thought about this. His birthright made him the leader of their family when they became grownups. That was several years away. He was hungry now. Did he really need to be the leader and get all of the family's valuables?

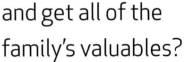

"You have a trade," said Esau.

"One bowl of stew, coming right up!" said Jacob. Jacob was excited. He really wanted to be in charge of their family.

The Blessing
Genesis 27:1-46

Jacob and Esau got older, as did their parents, Isaac and Rebekah. Isaac thought, *I am an old man. It is time to give my blessing to Esau.*

"Esau, come here," Isaac called. Esau came to his father. "Please hunt and make my favorite food. Then I will give you my blessing," Isaac instructed.

Esau left in search of food. Rebekah had heard Isaac. She wanted Jacob to have the blessing because God told her that her youngest son would lead the family.

Rebekah called for Jacob. "I want you to have the blessing, Jacob," Rebekah said. She helped Jacob dress in a disguise so Isaac would believe that Jacob was Esau. Rebekah made Isaac's favorite stew and gave it to Jacob to take to Isaac.

Jacob went into Isaac's tent. "Who are you?" Isaac asked. "It's me, Esau," said Jacob, "here is your food." Isaac ate his food and then prayed a blessing over Jacob.

Esau returned to Isaac only to discover that Isaac had given the blessing to Jacob. Esau was angry.

How do you think Jacob and Rebekah felt? How do you think Isaac and Esau felt? Have you ever tried to force your own way instead of trusting God?

Jacob's Ladder
Genesis 28:10-22

Jacob was scared, so he ran away to his uncle's house. After a day of walking, Jacob was sleepy. He lay his head on a rock and fell fast asleep.

He dreamt about God. God said, "Jacob, I am always with you. You will be a blessing." Jacob woke up and knew that God was always with him.

Joseph and His Brothers
Genesis 37:1-36

Jacob married and had twelve sons. One of Jacob's sons was Joseph, and he was Jacob's favorite. Jacob gave Joseph a special robe. None of the brothers had a robe like that. It made Joseph's brothers angry.

Joseph's dreams made them even more angry. "I dreamt that we were all bundling grain. Your grain bundles bowed down to my grain bundle. I also dreamt that the sun, the moon, and the stars bowed down to me. It means that you will all bow down to me," said Joseph. None of his brothers wanted to bow down to him.

The brothers went out to the fields to herd the sheep. Jacob sent Joseph to check on them. The brothers saw Joseph and came up with a plan to get him out of their lives. They took his robe and threw him into a pit until some traveling traders came by. They sold Joseph to the traders.

What could the brothers have done differently?

Joseph in Egypt
Genesis 39:1–40:23

Joseph was sold and traveled with a camel caravan to Egypt.

When Joseph arrived in Egypt, he worked for a man named Potiphar.

Joseph was a good worker. Soon Potiphar saw what a good worker Joseph was. So Potiphar put Joseph in charge of everything in Potiphar's house.

Potiphar's wife did not get along with Joseph. Potiphar's wife took Joseph's garment, showed it to her husband, and said, "Joseph keeps bothering me, and look, he left his clothing in our house!"

Potiphar threw Joseph in jail. The jailer grew to like and to trust Joseph, and the jailer put Joseph in charge of the jail. While Joseph was in jail, he began to tell the other prisoners what their dreams meant. One man was Pharaoh's cupbearer. His job was to bring Pharaoh drinks when Pharaoh was thirsty. The other man was Pharaoh's baker. His job was to bake Pharaoh good things to eat.

One morning Joseph overheard the men talking. They both had strange dreams. "I can help you understand your dreams," Joseph told the men. "Just tell me about them, and God will help me understand them."

The cupbearer began, "I dreamt that I made juice from grapes and gave it to Pharaoh. Pharaoh drank the juice. What does it mean?"

"Pharaoh will forgive you," said Joseph.

The baker told Joseph his dream, "I baked bread for Pharaoh, but birds came and ate all of the bread before I could give it to Pharaoh. What does it mean?"

"It means that Pharaoh will not forgive you," explained Joseph.

Joseph was right! A few days later, the dreams came true.

What do you think is the most important part of this story?

Joseph Saves the Day
Genesis 41:1-57

Two years had gone by since Joseph had helped the cupbearer and the baker with their dreams. Joseph was still in jail.

Meanwhile, Pharaoh was having strange dreams. No one was able to help him understand them. The cupbearer remembered Joseph's help and told Pharaoh about him. "Send for Joseph at once," ordered Pharaoh.

Have you ever had a strange dream? What happened?

Joseph was brought from the jail to Pharaoh's palace. "I need your help understanding my dreams, Joseph," said Pharaoh. "With God's help, I can help you to understand them," replied Joseph. "Please tell me your dreams."

"I dreamt that I saw seven fat cows grazing by the Nile River. All of a sudden, seven skinny cows appeared and ate the fat cows! It was strange and a little scary."

"Your dream is about what will happen. Egypt will have lots of food for seven years, then Egypt will have seven years without food. People will go hungry," Joseph explained.

"Joseph, I want you to help Egypt. You will be a leader and will help us store up food so we won't go hungry," decided Pharaoh. Joseph did help Egypt.

Joseph and His Brothers Reunited *Genesis 42:1–46:34*

The famine in Canaan was very, very bad. Jacob and his sons and their families were starving. They needed food. What should they do?

Jacob sent his sons to Egypt to buy some food. The brothers had to ask Joseph for food—the brother they had sold long ago—but they did not know it was him.

Joseph was the governor of Egypt, and he was very powerful. Joseph gave his brothers food, but he told them to bring their youngest brother, Benjamin, back to see him.

A few years later, Jacob's family in Canaan became hungry once again. The brothers went back to Egypt to buy more food. This time, they took their youngest brother, Benjamin, with them.

When the brothers stood in front of Joseph and asked for more food, Joseph said, "Go to my house, and we will eat together at noon." The brothers ate a feast with Joseph. Joseph knew they were his brothers, but they did not know that Joseph was their brother.

The brothers were given grain to put in their sacks.

Joseph told one of his servants to hide a cup in Benjamin's sack. After the brothers had traveled home for awhile, the servant went after them and said, "You have stolen Joseph's cup!"

Joseph said to his brothers, "Because you have stolen my cup, you must leave Benjamin here with me!"

Judah begged Joseph to let Benjamin go home with them.

Finally, Joseph cried and told his brothers who he really was. Joseph invited his brothers and their families to live in Egypt where there was plenty of food! Joseph's family did well, and they were happy for a while in the land of Egypt.

Joseph forgave. Is there someone you need to forgive?

Exodus

The word *exodus* means "the way out," and the miraculous escape known as the Exodus is considered one of the Bible's most important events. Exodus shows how God powerfully rescued the Israelites from slavery in Egypt and formed them into a new nation of Israel.

Tips for Adults

In the Book of Genesis, Jacob's family traveled to Egypt to have access to food. Hundreds of years later, that small family had grown into a large group of people called the Israelites. Egypt's king, Pharaoh, was so afraid the Israelites would cause him trouble that he forced them to become slaves. God saw their suffering and sent Moses to tell Pharaoh to set the Israelites free.

The Baby in the Basket
Exodus 1:8-14; 2:1-10

Many years ago, in a land called Egypt, a baby boy was born. His name was Moses. Moses' parents and his big sister, Miriam, loved him very much. Moses' parents were slaves and were forced to work very hard. The king of Egypt, Pharaoh, did not want the slaves to have many children, but Moses' mother loved Moses and she kept him safe.

One day Moses' mother made a special basket for him. She made it so that it would float in water and not sink. Moses' mother laid Moses in the basket and put it in the Nile River. She hid him behind some tall grasses so no one could see Moses. Miriam, Moses' older sister, was nearby and watched him in the basket. She could see anything that might happen to baby Moses.

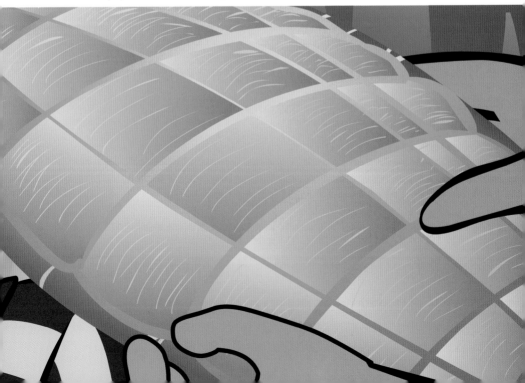

Soon, one of the pharaoh's daughters went to the river to take a bath. The pharaoh's daughter saw Moses' basket floating in the tall grass in the river. The princess went over to the basket and opened it. She saw baby Moses. He was crying, and she felt sorry for the baby.

Moses' sister, Miriam, saw what was happening. She ran to the pharaoh's daughter who was holding Moses. "Would you like me to get a woman to take care of the baby?" asked Miriam. The pharaoh's daughter said, "Yes, please do."

Miriam ran to get her mother and brought her to the pharaoh's daughter. The pharaoh's daughter handed baby Moses to his own mother and said, "Take care of this baby." Moses' mother took him home. When he was old enough, Moses' mother took him to the pharaoh's daughter, who adopted him and raised him in the pharaoh's house.

What do you think is the most important part of the story?

The Burning Bush

Exodus 2:11–3:22

Moses grew up into an adult. He saw the way the Egyptians were treating the Israelites as slaves. Moses did not like the way the Egyptians were hurting the Israelites—Moses' people. Moses got mad and scared, so he ran away to Midian.

Moses lived in Midian for many years. He got married and became a dad. He was a shepherd and cared for sheep.

One day Moses was taking care of the sheep on the edge of the desert near God's mountain. God appeared to Moses as a burning bush. Moses saw the flames on the bush, but the bush didn't burn. Moses got close to the bush and God called out to him, "Moses! I am God. I have seen my people as slaves in Egypt and have heard their cries. I know their pain. I have come to rescue them. I am sending you, Moses, to set my people free."

"Who am I to do that?" asked Moses.

"I will be with you, Moses," said God. "You will go to the Israelites and tell them that the Great I Am has sent you to free them from Egypt. You will go to the pharaoh and tell him to set the Israelites free. I will help you, Moses."

What do you think Moses was feeling when this happened?

Moses and Pharaoh

Exodus 5:1–13:9

Moses asked God for help speaking to the Israelites and to Pharaoh, so God suggested that Moses ask his brother, Aaron, to help.

Moses and Aaron went to see Pharaoh. They said, "God has sent us to tell you to let the people go!"

Pharaoh was stubborn and refused to let the people go. To force Pharaoh to set the Israelites free, God sent plagues to Egypt. God turned the water in the Nile River into blood. God sent frogs to Egypt. God sent lice to Egypt. God sent insects to Egypt. God sent diseases to the animals in Egypt. God sent ash that caused people to get skin sores to Egypt. God made it hail and thunder on Egypt. God sent locusts to Egypt. God took away the light in Egypt and made everything very dark.

Pharaoh still would not let the people be free from slavery. It was a sad day when their firstborn child had to die. That broke Pharaoh's heart.

Pharaoh finally said, "Go!" The Israelites were free.

And God's people were on the run.

How does God get your attention?

Crossing the Sea
Exodus 13:17–14:31

The people were so happy. Pharaoh said they could go. They packed up all their things. They were going to the new land that God had promised them.

But Pharaoh changed his mind. He did not want the people to go. He sent his army to catch them.

God's people came to the Reed Sea. How were they going to get to the other side? They were afraid. The king's army was behind them. The water was in front of them.

What do you think God's people were thinking when the Reed Sea parted?

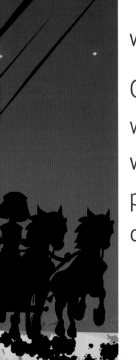

"Do not be afraid," said Moses. "God will help us."

God sent a strong wind to blow the water out of the way. God's people walked across on dry land. God's people were safe. Pharaoh's army could not chase them anymore.

Songs of Joy
Exodus 15:1-21

Miriam, Moses' sister, sang, "Sing to the Lord!" She was happy! God's people were happy! God helped them cross the Reed Sea. Now the people were safe.

Miriam was so happy that she wanted to sing and dance! She wanted to thank God for taking care of them.

Miriam sang, "Sing to the Lord!" and played music on her tambourine.

Then Miriam and all her friends played their tambourines as they sang together, "Sing to the Lord!"

What do you do when you are happy?

In the Wilderness
Exodus 15:22–17:7

The Israelites were free from Egypt, but now they were camping in the desert. The people wondered how they would live in the desert, away from their homes.

The people were unhappy. So they started complaining to their leader, Moses, "Why did you lead us into the desert?" They grumbled, "We're hungry, and there's no food to eat."

"Stop grumbling," said Moses. "God is with us, and God knows what we need."

That evening quail flew into the camp. The people caught the quail and cooked them for dinner. Everyone had enough to eat.

The next morning when the people came out of their tents, they saw thin, flaky stuff all over the ground. The people called the flakes *manna*, and they ate it like bread.

"Only gather as much manna as you can eat today," said Moses. "Don't try to keep any of it for tomorrow. God will give us enough for each day."

But some of the people didn't listen to Moses. They gathered more manna than they could eat and tried to keep the leftovers for later. But the leftover manna became infested with worms! So the people learned to gather just enough manna to eat each morning.

But the people were still not happy. They started complaining again. "We're thirsty," said the people. "We don't have anything to drink."

Who provides you with the things you need?

"Stop your complaining," said Moses. "God is with us, and God will make sure we have water to drink."

Then God told Moses to take his staff and go to a place called Horeb. Moses struck a rock with the staff. Fresh water started coming out of the rock!

So God provided food and water for the people in the wilderness.

Ten Commandments
Exodus 19:1–20:21

Moses and the people continued to move around in the wilderness. One day they came to a tall mountain. They set up their tents at the bottom of the mountain.

"I want the people to know that I am their God," God said to Moses. "Come to the top of the mountain, and I will give you special rules to help the people live together the way I want them to live."

So Moses went up the mountain while all the people waited below. The people saw the top of the mountain become covered with smoke. They heard thunder and saw lightning. The people were afraid.

Love God more than anything.

Don't let there be anything that takes the place of God.

Only use God's name with respect.

Rest on the seventh day.

Honor your father and mother.

Then God spoke these words:

1. There is only one God.

2. Worship only God.

3. Always say God's name with love.

4. Remember to rest one day a week.

5. Love your parents.

6. Do not kill.

7. Always love the person you marry.

8. Do not take what belongs to someone else.

9. Do not tell lies about other people.

10. Do not want something that someone else has.

Don't hurt others.

Be loyal to your husband or wife.

Don't take anything that doesn't belong to you.

Always be honest.

Never wish for something someone else has.

Then Moses came back down the mountain. He saw that the people were afraid.

"Don't be afraid," Moses said to the people. "The smoke and thunder help us remember how powerful God is. Listen to these special rules from God."

And the people listened as Moses told them God's rules.

? What other rules should we follow to show love to God and to each other?

A House for God

Exodus 25–31:15; 35:4–40:38

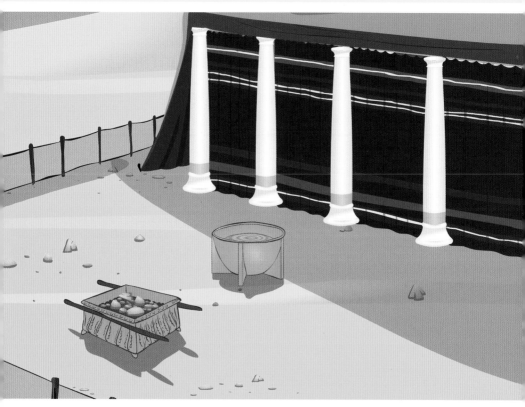

nce again Moses went up the mountain to talk to God. "Moses," said God, "I want the people to build a special place to worship me."

Everyone had a special job to do. Some of the people were builders. They made beautiful chests and tables out of wood. Then they covered the wood with gold.

Some of the people could sew. They made curtains out of purple and blue cloth. Some people made special clothing for the priests to wear.

God told them to make a special gold box called the sacred chest or the ark of the covenant. They put the special rules called the Ten Commandments inside the box.

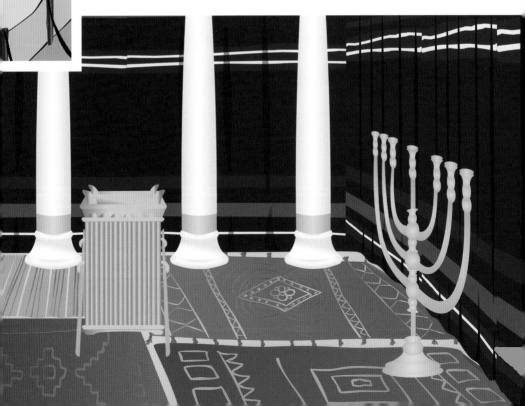

People also brought gifts to use in building the special place to worship God. Some people brought gold and silver. The gold and silver was used to make beautiful things for the place of worship.

Some people brought sweet-smelling spices. The spices would be used to make the place of worship smell good.

The place of worship was called the Tabernacle. It was like a very large tent.

Every time the people moved to a new place, they took the Tabernacle with them. The place of worship reminded the people that God was with them.

Do you have a special place where you go to worship God?

Joshua

Joshua tells the story of God's people crossing the Jordan River and entering the land God had led them to. This book is named for its main character, Joshua, who was brave and obeyed God.

Tips for
Adults

The Book of Joshua tells the stories of battles for the Promised Land. After many years of wandering in the wilderness, God's people were finally permitted to cross the Jordan River and enter the Promised Land. Their story reminds us to always listen to God and to be brave.

God Chooses Joshua
Joshua 1:1-9

Moses had led the people in the wilderness for over forty years. The people were finally ready to cross over into the land that God had promised. Moses stood before the people. He told them that a new leader had been chosen to take the people into the land.

"I have been your leader for many, many years," Moses said to the people. "But now it's time for a change. You need a new leader. So God picked Joshua to be your new leader."

"Be brave and strong," Moses said to Joshua. Then Moses helped Joshua understand how to be a good leader.

After Moses died, God spoke to Joshua.
"Get ready to go into the new land,"
said God. "I will help you the same way I
helped Moses."

"Be brave and strong," said God. "Obey all the things that Moses taught you. Don't be afraid. I will be with you wherever you go."

? What kind of leader will you be?

Spies in Canaan
Joshua 2:1-24

Joshua was going to lead the people into the land that would be their home. There was a city named Jericho in the new land. Joshua wanted to know more about the city, but Jericho was surrounded by a big wall.

Joshua called two men to a meeting. "Go into Jericho," said Joshua. "Spy on the people. Tell me what the city is like."

The two spies crept to the wall of Jericho. There was a gate in the wall, but the gate was guarded by the king's men. The king's men would never let in two spies! So the

spies climbed over the wall.

Once the two spies were in the city, they looked all around. They saw a house that was built right on the wall. The house belonged to a woman named Rahab.

The men went to Rahab's house. Rahab helped the spies. She told them all about Jericho.

When the king of Jericho heard that the spies had talked to Rahab, he sent guards to Rahab's house. Rahab had the spies lie down on her roof. Then she covered them up with stalks of grain. When the guards searched Rahab's house, they did not see men hiding under the grain.

After the guards went away, Rahab let the men climb down a rope out of her window. The window was in the wall that went around Jericho.

Before they left, Rahab asked the men to protect her and her family when they came back to Jericho.

? **Where is your favorite hiding place?**

"Tie a red rope in your window," said the spies. "Then we will know which house is yours. We will help you and your family because you have helped us."

The spies left Jericho and went safely back to Joshua.

Crossing the Jordan
Joshua 3:1-17; 4:1-24

Everyone was excited. The people were finally moving to the new land. The priests led the way, carrying the special chest that held God's rules, the Ten Commandments.

Everyone followed the priests until they came to the Jordan River. Then everyone stopped. The river was flooded. It was too deep for the people to cross. The people didn't know what to do.

"Trust God," Joshua said to the people. "I know God will do wonderful things for us."

Then Joshua told the priests to step into the river. As soon as the priests' feet touched the water, a dry path appeared. All the people crossed through the river on dry land.

Joshua told twelve men to each pick up a stone as they crossed the river. Joshua used the stones to build a monument.

"The monument will help us remember how God helped us cross the river," said Joshua.

Jericho
Joshua 6:1-27

W hat a big wall!" said the people. "It goes all around the city. How will we ever get into the city of Jericho?"

"God has a plan," said Joshua. "We must obey God and do what God tells us to do."

That's what the people did. First, all the soldiers lined up. Then seven priests with trumpets came next. The priests walked in front of the sacred chest that held God's rules, the Ten Commandments. More soldiers followed, making a huge

parade. The parade marched around the wall once a day for six days. The priests blew the trumpets as the people marched.

Then on the seventh day, God told the people to walk around the city wall seven times. Everyone was to march quietly until Joshua said to shout.

When the people marched around the wall for the seventh time, the priests blew the trumpets. Then Joshua said, "Shout!" and the wall around the city came crashing down. Joshua and the people rushed over the broken wall and took over the city.

Joshua sent the two men who had been spies to find Rahab. The men brought Rahab and her family to Joshua. Joshua made sure Rahab and her family were safe.

How do you think the people of Jericho felt when they saw the wall fall down?

Ruth

The Book of Ruth tells us how families take care of each other. The story has a sad beginning and a happy ending. At the start, a woman named Ruth and her mother-in-law, Naomi, are hungry and lonely. As their story unfolds, they find not only food, but friendship and love.

Tips for Adults

The story takes place before Israel had kings. Israel's tribes were facing a famine (that means there was no food), so Naomi, her husband, and their two sons moved to a new place called Moab. While there, Naomi's sons got married. Eventually, Naomi's husband and her sons died. Naomi and one of her daughters-in-law, Ruth, moved back to Israel together. Ruth promised to stay with Naomi no matter what.

Goodness
Book of Ruth

Naomi lived in the country of Moab. She had a husband and two sons. Ruth and Orpah were married to Naomi's sons and were her daughters-in-law.

One day Naomi's husband and two sons died. The women were very sad. Naomi decided to go back to her family in Bethlehem.

Before Naomi left Moab, she told her daughters-in-law to go back to live with their families. Orpah returned to her family, but Ruth would not leave Naomi.

Ruth said to Naomi, "Wherever you go, I will go. Your God will be my God."

Soon, Naomi and Ruth were on their way.

In Bethlehem, Ruth worked in a field and gleaned and gleaned. Ruth worked in the field of a man named Boaz. He liked Ruth.

Ruth took care of Naomi by picking up the leftover grain in Boaz's field and using it to make food. How can you care for someone you love?

Boaz married Ruth, and soon they had a baby boy. His name was Obed, but people called him, "Naomi's boy."

Ruth and Naomi were two happy women. They thanked God for the new life they had been given.

1 Samuel

First Samuel is named after Samuel, the main character of the first stories of this book. First Samuel explains the history of Israel from the time of the boy Samuel to Israel's first two kings. It tells exciting stories of Samuel, Saul, and David.

Tips for Adults

Before Samuel was born, his mother promised he would serve God his whole life. As Samuel grew older, he shared God's messages with God's people. This book reminds us that God is in charge, even when people demand their own king.

Hannah Prays
1 Samuel 1:1-28

Hannah and her husband, Elkanah, traveled to the temple in Shiloh to worship God. Hannah was very sad because she did not have any children. While they were in Shiloh, Hannah decided to go to the temple to pray.

Hannah prayed, "Dear God, I am so sad. I want a baby more than anything in the whole world. Please remember me and give me a baby boy to love and care for. If you give me a baby boy, I will bring him to the temple to learn all about you. I will teach my baby how to serve you all the days of his life."

Hannah prayed with her heart, her body, her lips, her breath, and with all of her might. Hannah knew that God would hear her prayers.

Hannah didn't know that Eli, the priest in charge of the temple, had been watching her. Eli said to Hannah, "Go in peace. I pray God answers your prayers."

Hannah and her family went back home. Hannah's prayer was soon answered. Hannah was going to have a baby!

Hannah and Elkanah had a baby boy. They named their baby, Samuel. Hannah kept her promise to God and raised Samuel to love and serve God all of his life.

Have you ever loved and cared for a baby?

God Calls Samuel
1 Samuel 3:1-21

A voice called out in the night, "Samuel, Samuel!" Samuel woke up. *Eli the priest is calling me*, thought Samuel.

Samuel went to where Eli was sleeping. "Eli, I'm here," said Samuel. "Why did you call me?"

"I didn't call you," said Eli. "Go back to bed."

So Samuel went back to bed. Samuel lay down on his mat and went back to sleep.

"Samuel, Samuel!" the voice called again. Samuel woke up. *Eli the priest must be calling me,* thought Samuel.

Samuel went to where Eli was sleeping. "Eli, I heard you call me," said Samuel.

"I didn't call you," said Eli. "Go back to bed."

So Samuel went back to bed. Samuel lay down on his mat and went back to sleep.

"Samuel, Samuel!" the voice called a third time.

Samuel woke up. *I'm sure Eli is calling me,* thought Samuel.

Samuel went to where Eli was sleeping. "Eli, I know I heard you call me this time," said Samuel.

"No," said Eli. "I didn't call you. You're hearing God call you. Go back to bed. If you hear the voice again, say, 'Speak, Lord. Your

servant is listening.'"

So Samuel went back to bed.

Samuel lay down on his mat and went back to sleep.

"Samuel, Samuel!" God called to Samuel.

Samuel woke up. This time Samuel knew God was calling him. "Speak, Lord. Your servant is listening," said Samuel. And Samuel listened to God.

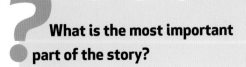
What is the most important part of the story?

Samuel Anoints Saul
1 Samuel 7:15–8:22; 10:17-24

Samuel the boy grew and grew. As Samuel grew, he served God.

When Samuel grew to be a man, he became a judge. Samuel helped the people know what God wanted them to do. Samuel served God his whole life.

"We want a king! We want a king!"
the people shouted to Samuel.

"You don't need a king," said Samuel. "God
is your leader."

"But all the other countries have kings,"
said the people. "We want to be like them."

"You won't really like
having a king," said
Samuel. "A king will
make your sons serve
in his army. A king will
make your daughters
cook his food. A king
will make you pay
money to him."

"We do want a king!" said the people.

So Samuel told God that the people wanted a king. God listened to Samuel and agreed to choose a king for the people.

God told Samuel to choose a young man named Saul as the first king.

Samuel called all the people to come together to see their new king. But when the people looked for Saul, they couldn't find him! He was hiding behind the big baskets and jars filled with supplies.

The people ran and found Saul.

"God has chosen Saul to be your king," said Samuel.

? How do you think Samuel felt in this story?

Samuel Anoints David
1 Samuel 16:1-23

Saul disobeyed God. The people needed a new king. God chose the new king from Jesse's sons. God sent Samuel to Bethlehem to find the new king.

Samuel arrived in Bethlehem and met Jesse's sons. Samuel thought the oldest son, Eliab, looked like the next king. But God told Samuel, "Do not look at his outward appearance. He is not the new king. Humans see only the outside of people. I look into the hearts of people."

Jesse presented each of his sons, but God said no to all of them.

"God hasn't chosen any of these sons to be the next king. Are these all of your sons?" Samuel asked Jesse.

"The youngest is out tending the sheep," said Jesse.

"Please send for him," said Samuel.

The youngest son, David, came in from the sheep. God said, "That is the one. Anoint him."

Samuel took the horn of oil and anointed David to be the next king.

How do you think David felt in this story?

David the Musician
1 Samuel 16:14-23

King Saul had nightmares at night and unhappy thoughts during the day. This made King Saul angry. King Saul's servants were worried about Saul. They wanted him to feel better. "Find me a musician!" King Saul snapped.

"I have heard that one of Jesse's sons is a good musician. He also loves God," said the servant.

The servant traveled to Bethlehem where Jesse and his sons lived. "Hi, Jesse. King Saul has bad thoughts. King Saul has requested your son the musician to come play for him," said the servant.

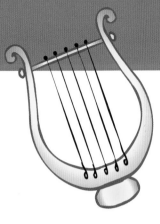

"David!" Jesse called out. David was out taking care of the family sheep. David came in from the field. Jesse told David about King Saul. David gathered his lyre while Jesse loaded up a donkey. David and the servant traveled back to King Saul.

When David began to play for King Saul, King Saul felt better. King Saul liked having David around. Anytime King Saul began to get upset, David would take out his lyre and play a pretty song for him. King Saul would always feel better.

What makes you feel better?

David and Goliath
1 Samuel 17:1-51a

The giant warrior named Goliath shouted, "Who will fight me?"

Goliath was King Saul's enemy. He was a very big man. He was over nine feet tall! King Saul and everyone in his army were afraid of Goliath. No one wanted to fight the very big man. King Saul and his army did not know what to do.

David was the youngest of eight sons. His three oldest brothers were in Saul's army. David stayed home, watching over the family's sheep.

"David," said his father, "take this food to your brothers. Find out what is happening with King Saul's army." So David took bread and cheese to his brothers in King Saul's army.

When David arrived at the camp, he saw Goliath. "Will no one fight me? Are all of you too afraid?" shouted Goliath.

"I'm not afraid," said David. "I'll fight Goliath."

"You?" said King Saul. "You can't fight such a big man. You are too small!"

"I take care of my father's sheep," said David. "I protect them from lions and bears. I can fight the big man just like I fight the lions and bears. I know God will be with me."

"Go ahead," said King Saul, "but wear my armor."

But when he put on King Saul's armor, he couldn't move!

"I can't wear your armor. It is too big for me," said David. So David took off the armor and got his slingshot.

Talk with your child about other ways David, King Saul, and the Israelites could have handled this experience with Goliath. What creative ways can we use when people are bullying us?

He found five smooth stones and put them in his shepherd's

David trusted God would be with him. That made him brave. Have you ever been brave?

bag. Then he went to meet Goliath.

The very big man saw the small shepherd boy coming toward him. "Why, they have sent a boy to fight me!" laughed Goliath.

"I'm not afraid of you. I know God is with me," said David. Then David put a stone in his slingshot and slung it at Goliath.

The stone hit Goliath in the head. He fell down to ground. David, the small young shepherd boy, won the fight against the very big Goliath.

David and Jonathan
1 Samuel 18:1-5; 20:1-42

David and Jonathan lived in the king's palace. Jonathan was the king's son. David played the harp for the king.

David and Jonathan were friends. Jonathan wanted to show his friend, David, how much he cared about him. So Jonathan gave David his own robe to wear. He also gave David his sword, his bow, and his belt.

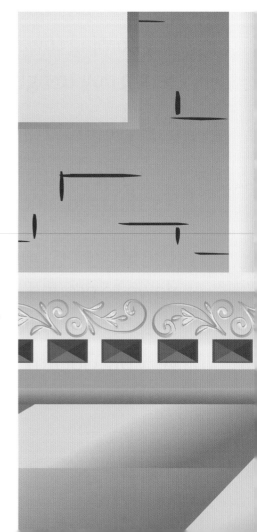

"We will always be friends," said Jonathan.

"Yes," promised David, "we will always be friends."

King Saul became worried that more people liked David than liked him. So King Saul became very angry with David.

David was afraid. "Jonathan," said David, "I think your father wants to hurt me."

"Oh, no," said Jonathan. "You've got to be wrong. My father knows that you are my best friend."

But David was still afraid. So David and Jonathan came up with a plan.

"I'll go see my father," said Jonathan, "while you hide. After I talk with him, I'll come back to you and let you know if you're safe."

So Jonathan went to see his father. When Jonathan talked about his friend, David, King

Saul got angry! Jonathan knew that David was right—his father wanted to hurt his friend. Jonathan knew he had to tell David.

Who are your good friends? Say a prayer for them.

Jonathan took his bow and arrow, and went to the field where David was hiding. Jonathan shot an arrow out into the field. The arrow went far from where David was hiding.

David knew that Jonathan was sending him a secret message. Because Jonathan shot the arrow far from where David was hiding, David knew he must run far from the king.

Even though David had to run from the king, David and Jonathan kept their promise to one another.

David and Abigail
1 Samuel 25:1-42

Nabal was very mean. David and his men were very hungry. When they asked Nabal to share his food with them, Nabal said no. That made David very angry. David and his men set off to teach Nabal a lesson.

When Nabal's wife, Abigail, heard about David's intention to teach Nabal a lesson, she made a plan to stop the fight. Abigail loaded up lots of food to share with David and his men. Abigail would share the food David had asked for.

"David, please don't be angry anymore! Here is some food. Please don't start a fight," Abigail said to David. David didn't start a fight. He forgave Nabal for being mean. Abigail was a great peacemaker!

How might things have gone if Nabal had been kind to David from the beginning?

2 Samuel

Second Samuel continues the history of Israel that began in 1 Samuel. It tells the rest of the story of King David's life. Second Samuel contains stories of both good and bad choices David made during his many years as the king of Israel.

Tips for
Adults

Second Samuel begins where 1 Samuel ends. Saul has died, and David is crowned the king of Israel. As Israel's new king, David made Israel a strong nation. But this book reminds us that even the best leaders disobey God or have problems. Even then, God forgives.

David Dances
2 Samuel 6:1-19

King David was bringing the chest of God to the city. The chest was very special. It reminded the people that God was with them.

"Praise God!" shouted King David.

King David was very happy that he could bring the chest of God home. He was so happy that he planned a big parade so everyone could see the chest.

Many, many people joined King David in the parade.

Some people played trumpets to praise God. Some people played harps to praise God. Other people sang to praise God, but King David wanted to praise God with his whole body. So King David danced!

"Praise God!" he shouted. "Praise God!"

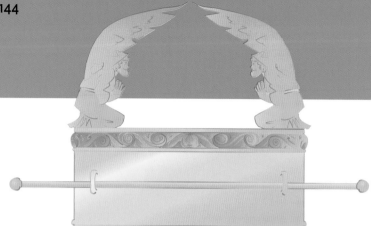

The parade ended when the chest of God was carried into the city.

"God bless you," King David said to the people. "Remember that God will be with you your whole lives."

Then King David gave bread and date cakes and raisin cakes to all the people.

King David knew it was a great way to praise God!

How do you like to praise God?

Kindness
2 Samuel 9:1-13

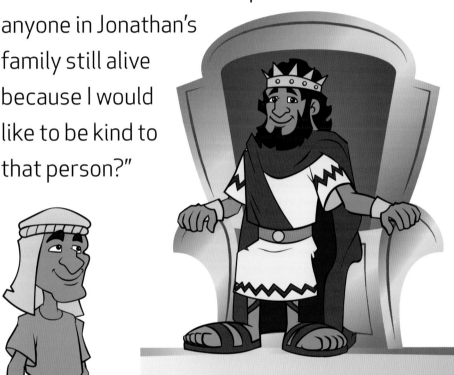

King David was thinking about his best friend, Jonathan, who had died. King David asked one of his helpers, "Is there anyone in Jonathan's family still alive because I would like to be kind to that person?"

Say it!

Mephibosheth
mi-fib' oh-sheth

David's helper said, "Jonathan has a son whose name is Mephibosheth."

King David asked some of his helpers to find Mephibosheth and bring Mephibosheth back to him.

When the helpers brought Mephibosheth to King David, he could see that Mephibosheth was afraid. King David said, "Don't be afraid. I want to be kind to you. Your father, Jonathan, and I were good friends. I would like you to eat with me at my table."

King David invited Mephibosheth
to eat with him always, and he gave
Mephibosheth everything that
had belonged to Mephibosheth's
grandfather.

**How do you think
Mephibosheth felt in
the story?**

1 Kings

First Kings tells the stories of Solomon and the kings who ruled after him. Solomon didn't always obey God. Because of this, the kingdom of Israel split into two kingdoms: Judah and Israel.

Tips for Adults

First Kings continues the long story started in 1 and 2 Samuel. It tells of Israel's history from King Solomon to King Ahab. It also explains how the nation of Israel divided into two kingdoms, Judah in the south and Israel in the north. Each kingdom had a different king. Some kings loved God, but most kings disobeyed.

Solomon Becomes King
1 Kings 2:1-4; 3:1-15

One night while Solomon was sleeping, God spoke to Solomon in a dream. "Solomon, ask me for whatever you want," said God.

Solomon prayed, "You have been good to me, and made me the king of Israel."

Solomon continued, "I am still young, and I need your help in everything. Please give me wisdom so I can be a good king."

God was very happy that Solomon asked for wisdom. "I will give you the wisdom and understanding you have asked for," said God. "Because your heart's desire is good, I will also bless you."

Solomon asked God for wisdom. What would you ask God for?

Solomon Builds the Temple
1 Kings 6:1-38

Solomon wanted to do something to show the people that God was with them. So Solomon built the Temple, a special place where the people could come to worship God.

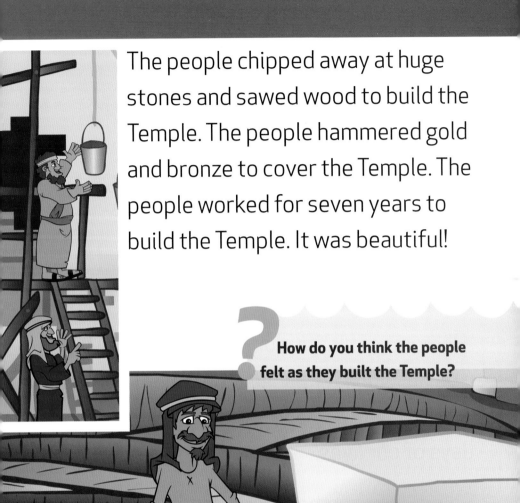

The people chipped away at huge stones and sawed wood to build the Temple. The people hammered gold and bronze to cover the Temple. The people worked for seven years to build the Temple. It was beautiful!

?

How do you think the people felt as they built the Temple?

After the Temple
was finished,
Solomon gathered
all the people together. The
priests moved the chest of
God into the Temple.

Solomon stood in front of all the people.

"Remember all the wonderful things
God has done for us," said Solomon.
"Remember that God is with us all the
days of our lives."

Solomon knew the Temple would help
the people remember that God was with
them.

The Temple was finished. It was a special
place for the people to gather together
and worship God.

Solomon Dedicates the Temple
Kings 8:1-66

It was time to move the sacred chest to the new Temple in Jerusalem. So Solomon called all of the Israelite leaders together.

When the leaders arrived, the priests carried the sacred chest and all of the holy things into the inner holy place of the Temple. God's presence and glory filled the Temple.

Solomon knelt down at
the altar to pray, saying, "I
have built God a house to live in forever.
Bless God! There is no god like you. God,
you keep your promises. Please listen
to your people when they pray in the
Temple. Care for every person."

Solomon stood up and faced the leaders. He said, "May God be blessed! God has cared for us. We will live the way God wants us to."

How do you think Solomon felt as he prayed to God?

Elijah and the Ravens
1 Kings 16:29-30; 17:1-7

There was a man named Elijah who lived in the land of Israel. Elijah was a prophet. A prophet speaks up when things are unfair and helps people know what God wants them to do. Elijah tried to warn King Ahab that there was going to be a drought, and there would be no water or food for many years. But the king would not listen to Elijah.

Soon, it stopped raining, and the creeks dried up. There was no water to drink nor food to eat. God told Elijah to go across the Jordan River and live near Cherith Brook. God said, "I will send raven birds to bring you food."

Elijah obeyed God. Every day, ravens brought him bread and meat, and Elijah drank water from Cherith Brook.

How does God care for you?

Elijah and the Prophets
1 Kings 18:20-39

God came to Elijah and said, "Go before King Ahab! I will then send rain." So Elijah went to see King Ahab.

"You have caused trouble by following Baal instead of God. Gather all of the prophets of Baal to meet me on Mount Carmel," said Elijah to Ahab.

Elijah met all of the Israelites and the prophets of Baal on Mount Carmel. Elijah talked to all of the people, "If God is God, follow God. If Baal is God, follow Baal. Let's offer God and Baal sacrifices. The god who answers with fire is the true God."

The prophets of Baal prepared the sacrifice for Baal. They called on Baal to bring fire, but nothing happened.

Elijah prepared the sacrifice for God. Elijah set up the altar, then poured a lot of water all over the sacrifice. Elijah prayed to God asking God to send fire. Fire came down from the sky and burned up the sacrifice and the altar! Everyone believed that God was God.

How do you think the people watching the prophets of Baal and Elijah felt in this story?

2 Kings

Second Kings continues the story that 1 Kings began. It tells of Israel's Northern and Southern Kingdoms, Israel and Judah. Each kingdom was defeated by war and their citizens taken as prisoners to distant lands.

Tips for Adults

After King David and King Solomon, the United Kingdom (Israel and Judah) broke into two parts: the Northern Kingdom of Israel and the Southern Kingdom of Judah. First Kings tells the story of these two kingdoms' earliest days. Second Kings tells the rest of the story. Second Kings shows us that God's people didn't always do what was right, and in the end, they were defeated by war and taken as prisoners to distant lands.

Faithfulness
2 Kings 22:1–23:23

Josiah was only eight years old when he became king of Judah. An eight-year-old boy is not very big, but King Josiah was a good king because he tried to do what God wanted.

Some years later, King Josiah ordered the Temple to be cleaned and fixed. King Josiah wanted the Temple to be a good place to worship God. One day while cleaning the Temple, the workers found a very old book called, *The Book of God's Law*. They took the book to King Josiah who read it. King Josiah became upset because he realized that the people had forgotten about God.

Sometimes the people forgot to worship God, and they worshipped other gods. Sometimes the people built buildings and altars for other gods. The people were not loving God and worshipping God like they should.

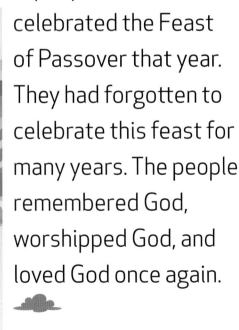

King Josiah decided to get rid of everything that the people should not worship. King Josiah said, "From now on, we will only worship the one true God!"

King Josiah and the people of Judah

celebrated the Feast of Passover that year. They had forgotten to celebrate this feast for many years. The people remembered God, worshipped God, and loved God once again.

? How do you show your faith in God?

Elisha and the Widow's Jars
2 Kings 4:1-7

One day a poor widow came to Elisha for help. Elisha was a prophet. A prophet speaks up when things are unfair and helps people know what God wants them to do. Her husband had died, and she did not have enough money to take care of her sons.

"What do you still have left in your house?" Elisha asked the woman.

"I just have one small jar of oil," said the woman.

"One jar of oil is enough," said Elisha. "Here's what I want you and your children to do: Go and find as many empty jars as you can. Look all over your house. Borrow empty jars from your neighbors. Get lots and lots of empty jars."

"Now," said Elisha, "go inside your house with your sons and close the door. Start pouring the oil from your one jar of oil into all the jars."

The woman and her sons carried the empty jars into the house and shut the door.

How do you think the woman felt when her small jar of oil kept filling more and more jars?

The woman filled one jar, then two jars, and then three jars. The woman kept filling jars until there were no more jars. Then the oil ran out.

The woman went back to Elisha. She told him what happened.

"Good!" said Elisha. "Sell the jars of oil to get the money you need to care for you and your sons."

And the woman did.

Elisha and the Servant Girl

2 Kings 5:1-19

A servant girl worked for the wife of a man named Naaman. Naaman was a general in the army of a country called Aram. Naaman was an important man, and he had a skin disease that made him feel miserable.

The servant girl knew about a prophet named Elisha. The servant girl told Naaman's wife that the prophet could heal Naaman's skin disease. Then Naaman's wife told Naaman what the servant girl had said.

Naaman and his servants traveled to see Elisha. When Elisha heard why Naaman was there, he sent a messenger out to meet the general.

"Go wash in the Jordan River seven times," the messenger told the important general.

Naaman got mad. "I've wasted my time," complained Naaman. "This Elisha didn't even bother to come out and see me himself. He just sent out a messenger. And why should I wash in the dirty water of this river? There are cleaner rivers where I live. I'm an important general. Washing in a river is too easy."

"But General Naaman," said the servants, "we know you can do hard things. Since the prophet Elisha gave you such an easy thing to do, why not try it?"

So Naaman went to the Jordan River and washed seven times. When Naaman came out of the river, his skin was healed.

Naaman went back to Elisha and told him that he now believed in God.

How do you think Naaman felt when he saw he was healed?

Esther

Esther is a thrilling story of a young Jewish woman chosen to be queen of Persia. When God's people were threatened with death, she bravely stood up for her people and saved their lives.

Tips for
Adults

Esther is one of the Bible's most dramatic stories. Persia's King Ahasuerus looks for a new queen, and a young Jewish woman, Esther, is chosen. Esther chose not to tell anyone that she was Jewish. She didn't know if people would like a Jewish queen. This book tells how Esther made a brave choice to tell the king that she was Jewish—and to ask him to save her people from death.

Courageous Queen
Book of Esther

Esther was very beautiful. She lived with her older cousin, Mordecai. Both Esther and Mordecai were Jews. They loved God and followed God's rules.

One day the king decided he wanted a new queen. Hundreds of beautiful women, including Esther, went to the palace to meet the king. When the king met Esther, he chose her. Esther went to live at the palace, but she didn't tell anyone that she and Mordecai were Jews.

The king had a helper named Haman. Haman didn't like Mordecai, and decided he would get rid of anyone that was a Jew like Mordecai. Haman tricked the king into making a law to kill all people who were Jews. The king agreed. Neither Haman nor the king knew that Esther was a Jew.

Queen Esther and Mordecai were very upset. They were Jewish. "You must help our people," Mordecai told Queen Esther. "You must talk to the king."

But Queen Esther was afraid. No one could see the king without the king saying it was all right to come. If she went to the king without his approval, Queen Esther could be killed. If the king held his scepter out to Queen Esther, she was safe. But if he didn't hold out his scepter, she would be killed.

"You must be brave," said Mordecai.

"I'll need help," said Queen Esther. "Have all our people pray that God will help me be brave."

Queen Esther went to the king. When the king saw Queen Esther, he held out his scepter. Queen Esther was safe!

The king asked her, "What is it you want, Queen Esther?"

"Please, come to dinner," said Queen Esther. "And bring Haman."

So the king and Haman went to eat with Queen Esther. At the dinner, Queen Esther told the king that she and Mordecai were Jews. Then she told the king that Haman wanted to kill all the Jews.

The king was very angry with Haman. He didn't want Queen Esther killed. And the king didn't want her people killed. The king got rid of Haman instead. The king made a new law that kept Queen Esther, Mordecai, and her people safe.

How do you think Esther felt in this story?

183

Psalms

Psalms has songs and hymns written by many different authors. Some songs are of praise and thanks, and some are about sadness. Others ask for help or forgiveness. Psalms help people talk with God and worship God.

Tips for Adults

There are 150 songs and hymns in Psalms. The themes in these songs touch on almost everything that happens in our lives. They tell of all kinds of human emotions—happiness, sadness, peace, anger, fear, and confidence. This book helps us worship God with songs during the highs and lows of our lives.

Gentleness
Psalm 23:1-6

God is like a shepherd. I am like God's sheep. God provides everything I need.

God is like a shepherd. I am like God's sheep. God leads me to good things because God is good.

God is like a shepherd. I am like God's sheep. I do not need to be afraid; God is always with me.

God is like a shepherd. I am like God's sheep. God's goodness and faithfulness will be with me always.

God is like a shepherd. I am like God's sheep. I will be with God all of my life.

God is like a shepherd. I am like God's sheep. We can trust God's love and care. God is great, indeed!

What else is God like?

Joy
Psalm 100:1-5

Worship the LORD with joy, and sing happy, happy songs!

God made us.
We belong to God.

Give thanks to God.
Give praise to God.

God is good;
God loves us forever.

What is your favorite song to sing?

Proverbs

A proverb is a small saying that contains a big truth, and the Book of Proverbs gives hundreds of these wise insights for every area of life. They can tell how to obey God, avoid pain, and enjoy success.

Tips for **Adults**

The Bible says that Solomon was the wisest man ever. His insight was God's answer to Solomon's prayer that he be able to tell the difference between good and evil. Much of the Book of Proverbs is said to be a collection of Solomon's wise sayings. Shorter sections are said to be written by other people. The wisdom in the Book of Proverbs helps us to listen, learn, and to think and act differently. Having wisdom helps us make good choices and do what is right.

Solomon's Wisdom Proverbs
Proverbs 6:6-8; 10:1; 17:17

King Solomon prayed to God for wisdom. He wanted to make good choices and lead God's people well. Some of the wise things Solomon taught are written down in the Book of Proverbs.

Solomon taught about working hard by telling a story about ants. He said, "Pay attention to ants. They work hard. Because of their hard work, they always have food. You should not be lazy, but hard-working like ants."

Solomon also said, "When you make good choices, your parents will be happy. When you make bad choices, your parents will be sad."

Solomon taught about how to be a good friend and family member. He said, "Friends love and care for each other all the time. Family members help when there is trouble."

What wise things have you been taught?

Isaiah

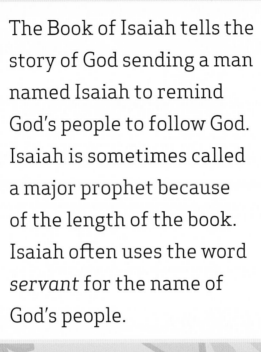

The Book of Isaiah tells the story of God sending a man named Isaiah to remind God's people to follow God. Isaiah is sometimes called a major prophet because of the length of the book. Isaiah often uses the word *servant* for the name of God's people.

Tips for
Adults

This book has three parts. Chapters 1–39 talk about serious problems with worship and government—how rich people were mistreating poor people. Chapters 40–55 address people who lived about two hundred years after the prophet Isaiah. They promise that God will bring God's people back to their homeland in Israel. Chapters 56–66 encourage and warn a generation who have returned to Israel.

The Peaceable Kingdom
Isaiah 11:6-9

A long time ago, God sent a message to the people. The message said that a little child would come and teach us how to live in peace.

When there is peace, a wolf can sit with a lamb. When there is peace, a cow and a lion can share their food without fighting. When there is peace, young bears and young cows can be friends and play together.

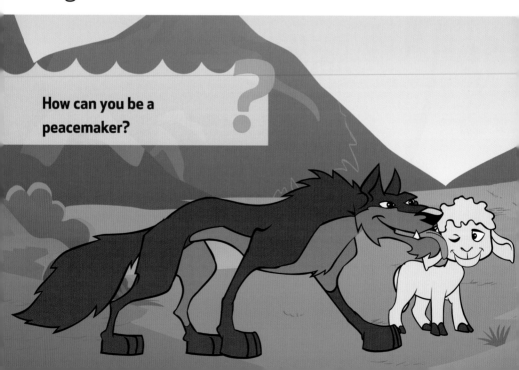

How can you be a peacemaker?

Jeremiah

The Book of Jeremiah is named for a prophet who looked around and saw the people of Judah disobeying God. He felt sad that God's people were not living the way God wanted them to live, but had hope for them.

Tips for Adults

The Book of Jeremiah begins with God sending Jeremiah to speak to the kingdom of Judah. Jeremiah cried because people dishonored God. He cried because people got hurt when they disobeyed God. Jeremiah felt so sad about God's people that he became known as "the weeping prophet." Jeremiah spoke about justice and mercy. He declared that God would change the hearts of God's people.

A Baby Is Coming
Jeremiah 23:5-8

"The time is coming," said Jeremiah, "when the Israelites will have a king from David's family. He will be a wise king, and he will do good things. While this king is alive, all the people will be safe. Even his name will help us remember that God is good."

How do you know that God is good?

Daniel

The Book of Daniel has some of the Bible's best-known stories. It tells how Daniel and others bravely obeyed God, even when facing lions and fire. The book was written to encourage God's people to be faithful to God, no matter what challenges lie before them.

Tips for **Adults**

The Book of Daniel begins with Daniel and his friends, Shadrach, Meshach, and Abednego, training to serve the king of Babylon. These four young men wanted to obey God in everything they did. Even when they were ordered to break God's instructions by the king, they refused. This book shows us how to be courageous, even when people dislike our faith in God.

Self-control
Daniel 1:1-21

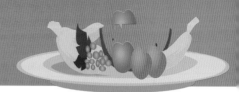

The king of Babylon was a powerful king. He became ruler over God's people. He made many of God's people move to Babylon, a country far away from their homes.

One day the king called for his most important helper. "I want you to choose several young men to be my helpers," said the king. "The young men must be smart and healthy. They'll live here at my palace and even eat my food."

The king's helper hurried to do what the king wanted him to do. He chose many young men, including Daniel and his three friends.

Many of the young men were pleased to live in the palace and eat the king's food. But Daniel and his friends knew that the king's food was not the kind of food God wanted them to eat.

"We cannot eat the king's food," said Daniel. "We follow God, so we must eat the food God wants us to eat."

The king's helper became worried. "But the king said you're to eat his food. If you don't eat it, I'll get in trouble!"

"Let me and my friends eat only vegetables for ten days," said Daniel. "Then you can see if we are as healthy as everyone else."

The king's helper agreed. Daniel and his friends ate only vegetables while the other young men ate the king's food.

When the ten days were up, the king's helper looked at Daniel and his friends.

"You're very healthy! You look even better than everyone else," said the king's helper.

God gave wisdom and knowledge to Daniel and his friends.

The four friends were chosen to serve in the king's palace.

? **How do you think it felt to be different than the rest of the helpers?**

Courageous Friends
Daniel 3:1-30

I want everyone in my kingdom to worship me," said the king. "I'm the most important person in the land."

So the king made a new rule. "Anytime the music plays," said the king, "everyone must stop what they're doing and kneel

down to the gold statue. Whoever does not worship the statue will be thrown into a very hot fire."

Three of the king's helpers were young men who believed in God. They knew that if they worshipped the gold statue, they would be obeying the king, but disobeying God. They decided that they would obey God. When the music played, they did not kneel and worship the statue.

The king found out that Shadrach, Meshach, and Abednego did not worship the gold statue. "If you kneel down and worship the statue the next time the music plays, you'll be safe," said the king. "If you don't, I'll throw you into a very hot fire."

"We won't worship a statue," said the three young men. "We only worship God."

"Make the fire even hotter!" yelled the king. He was very angry. "Then throw these three men into the fire!"

And so Shadrach, Meshach, and Abednego were thrown into the very hot fire. The king watched to see what would happen. He was surprised to see the men walking around in the fire. They were not hurt.

Then the king started counting, "One, two, three, four." Four? Why were there four men? "Didn't we put three men in the fire?" asked the king. "Now there are four!"

What a surprise! An angel was in the fire with Shadrach, Meshach, and Abednego.

"Let the men out," said the king.

The three young men came out of the fire. They were not hurt at all. They didn't even smell like fire.

"Look, their God took care of them," said the king. "Praise God!"

What do you think Shadrach, Meshach, and Abednego felt in this story?

Courageous Daniel
Daniel 6:1-28

Daniel loved God. Every day Daniel knelt down in front of his window and prayed to God. He prayed in the morning, he prayed at noontime, and he prayed in the evening.

Daniel worked for the king. He was a very good worker. Because Daniel was such a good worker, the king planned to make Daniel the boss of all the king's workers.

The king's other workers did not like Daniel. They wanted to get rid of Daniel. So the king's workers went to the king.

"Oh, great King," said the workers. "Everyone in your kingdom should know how great you are! We think you should make a new rule that everyone can pray only to you. If someone prays to anyone else, that person should be thrown into a den of hungry lions!"

The king was pleased that his workers thought he was so great. He liked the rule, and so it became a law.

"Everyone must pray to me for thirty days," said the king. "Anyone who doesn't follow this law will be thrown into a den of lions."

But Daniel loved God. So Daniel knelt down in front of his window and prayed to God, just like he did every day.

One of the king's workers saw Daniel praying to God. The worker told the king what Daniel was doing.

"Oh, no!" said the king. "Not Daniel. I don't want to put Daniel in the den of hungry lions!" But even the king had to follow the law.

"I hope your God will keep you safe," said the king as Daniel was thrown into the den of lions. That night the king was so worried about Daniel, he could not sleep.

The next morning, the king hurried to the den of lions. "Daniel, Daniel," cried the king. "Did your God save you from the lions?"

"I am safe!" shouted Daniel. "God closed the mouths of the hungry lions."

Daniel came out of the lions' den. The king was happy!

"I have a new law," said the king. "Everyone should pray to God like Daniel."

How do you think the king felt when he found Daniel alive with the lions?

Jonah

The Book of Jonah tells the story of a prophet who didn't want to obey God's command to preach to an enemy nation. When the prophet Jonah tried to escape God's order by taking a boat to a distant place, a great fish swallowed Jonah.

Tips for Adults

God told Jonah to preach a warning to the people of Nineveh, but Jonah didn't want to. Nineveh was the capital of Assyria, one of Israel's most frightening enemies. Jonah didn't want God to give the people of Nineveh a chance to stop making bad choices, so he ran away. But Jonah couldn't get far. Jonah made it to Nineveh and taught the people about God. The people believed! This book shows us that God is eager to love us all.

Jonah and the Fish
Book of Jonah

One day Jonah heard God speaking to him. "Jonah!" said God. "Listen to me. I want you to go to a city named Nineveh. Tell the people in that city to worship me."

"But God," whined Jonah, "I don't want to go to Nineveh."

So Jonah decided to run away. He found a ship that was sailing to a city that was far away from Nineveh. Jonah got on board the ship. Once he was on the ship, Jonah felt safe. He felt so safe, he went to sleep.

But the ship sailed right into a storm. The ship began to rock back and forth on the waves, but Jonah kept sleeping. The rain started to pound the deck of the ship, but Jonah kept sleeping. The sailors were afraid the ship was going to break apart, but Jonah kept sleeping.

"Jonah! Jonah!" cried the sailors. "Wake up! The ship is about to sink. Pray for help."

Jonah knew that the storm was his fault. He told the sailors to throw him into the sea.

So the sailors threw Jonah into the sea, and the storm stopped. Jonah went down into the sea.

Just then, God sent a very big fish to swallow Jonah. Jonah lived inside the belly of the fish for three days.

"God, I'm sorry," prayed Jonah from inside the fish. "I made a bad choice when I tried to run away from you. I promise that I will go to Nineveh and do what you want me to do."

The fish spit Jonah out onto dry land.

"Jonah!" said God. "Listen to me. I want you to go to a city named Nineveh. Tell the people in that city to worship me."

This time, Jonah went.

Jonah was afraid to tell the people of Nineveh that God loved them. Have you ever been afraid to do something? What did you do?

Matthew

The first four books of the New Testament, the Gospels, tell exciting stories about Jesus. Matthew is like a bridge between the Old and New Testaments. It shows how Jesus' teachings compare to the instruction God gave in the Old Testament.

Tips for Adults

The Book of Matthew was written at the end of the first century by an anonymous writer. Church tradition identified the writer as Matthew, but we don't know for sure. We do know that the author teaches the audience that Jesus is the Christ and the interpreter of the Jewish Scriptures. The author teaches us that Jesus came so people could experience God's kingdom.

Joseph's Story
Matthew 1:18-24

In the time before Jesus was born, there was a young man named Joseph. Joseph was engaged to marry a young woman named Mary. Joseph came from the family of King David.

Joseph learned that Mary was going to have a baby. One day Joseph had a dream. In the dream, he saw an angel of God. The angel said, "Joseph, the baby that Mary is having is God's gift to the whole world. Marry her. Name the baby, Jesus, Emmanuel, which means *God with us*."

Joseph did marry Mary. Joseph and Mary obeyed God. When Mary gave birth to a son, Joseph named him Jesus.

Follow the Star
Matthew 2:1-12

At the time when Jesus was born, in a faraway place there were wise men who spent their time watching the stars. One night they noticed a very special star in the sky. It was very bright and seemed to be moving ahead of them. The wise men studied their charts and decided this

special star must be the star that would lead them to the new king.

They wanted to bring special gifts to the new king. They packed frankincense, gold, and myrrh—gifts fit for a king—and set out following the star.

The Book of Matthew was written for a Jewish Christian audience. They would have been shocked that the first people to know about Jesus, the Jewish Messiah, were not Jewish! God's love is big enough for all of us.

The wise men arrived in Bethlehem, following the special star until it stopped over a little house.

When the wise men entered the house, they met the new king, Jesus, and his mom, Mary. The wise men knelt down and offered the new king their gifts of frankincense, gold, and myrrh.

How do you think the wise men felt on their long journey to meet Jesus?

Come to the River
Matthew 3:13-17

When Jesus grew up and was ready to begin his ministry, he went to the Jordan River to see John the Baptizer. John was baptizing people in the river. Jesus asked John to baptize him, but John tried to stop him. "I need to be baptized by you!" said John.

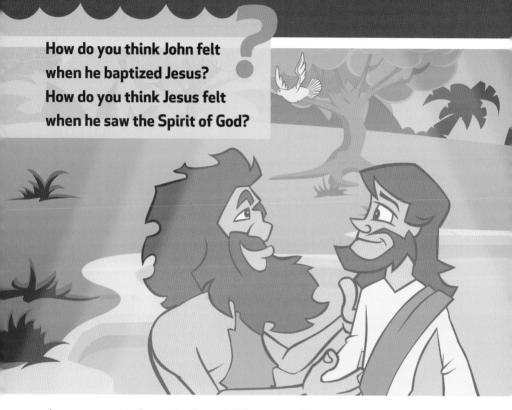

How do you think John felt when he baptized Jesus? How do you think Jesus felt when he saw the Spirit of God?

Jesus said to John, "Please baptize me. It is important for my ministry." So John agreed to baptize Jesus.

When Jesus came up out of the water, the heavens opened to him and he saw the Spirit of God come down like a dove on him. A voice from heaven said, "This is my Son. I love him. He makes me happy."

Jesus Calls the Fishermen
Matthew 4:18-22

One day Jesus was walking along the Galilean Sea when he saw two fishermen. One fisherman's name was Peter, and one fisherman's name was Andrew. Peter and Andrew were brothers. The brothers were fishing with their fishing net.

Jesus called out to Peter and Andrew, "Come, follow me! I will teach you how to fish for people."

Peter and Andrew left their nets and followed Jesus.

Jesus walked down the shore where he saw two more brothers, James and John, who were mending their nets with their father.

Jesus said to the men, "Come and follow me!"

James and John left the boat and their father, and followed Jesus.

Jesus calls us to follow him. What do you do as a follower of Jesus?

Peace
Matthew 5:1-9

One day Jesus saw a large crowd of people gathering to hear him teach. Jesus and his disciples went up a mountainside and sat down. The crowd of people came to him, and Jesus began to teach them.

Jesus taught the people in beatitudes. Beatitudes describe the here and now, and what will be. Jesus taught that even when we are sad, tired, hurt, grumpy, or grieving, we can have hope that things will get better.

How do you think the crowd felt when Jesus offered them this lesson?

Jesus said, "When you are sad, God will comfort you. When you are hurt by someone, God will make you feel better. Happy people make peace with other people. When you try to do the right thing and people make fun of you, God will help you. God will bless you, and you will truly be happy."

Have you ever felt very sad? What happened to make you feel better?

The Lord's Prayer
Matthew 6:5-15

Jesus continued teaching the large crowd on the mountainside. He said, "When you pray to God, pray like this:

> **If there is a version of the Lord's Prayer that you say at your church, pray that version of the prayer together.**

"God in heaven,
 your name is holy.
Let what happens in your kingdom
 happen on earth.
Give us everything we need.
Forgive us;
 help us forgive others.
Help us make good choices,
 instead of bad ones."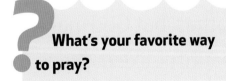

What's your favorite way to pray?

The Birds of the Air
Matthew 6:25-34

Jesus continued to teach the crowd on the mountainside. Jesus taught the people not to worry.

He said, "Don't worry about your life. Some of you are hungry, and some of you do not have much clothing. Don't worry about where you will get food or clothing.

"Look at the birds. They don't work like people do, but they do not worry about where they will get seeds. God feeds them.

"Look at the lilies. They don't make clothes, but God makes their petals beautiful, like dresses.

"God cares for each of you. God will provide for your needs. Don't worry," taught Jesus.

Sometimes worry can make us sad or mad. What calms you when you worry?

The Golden Rule
Matthew 7:12

Jesus continued to teach the crowd on the mountainside. He told the people a very special rule. The rule is so special, we call it the Golden Rule. This is what Jesus said: "Treat people in the same way that you want people to treat you."

That means that if we want people to be kind to us, we need to be kind to other people.

The Two Houses
Matthew 7:24-27

Jesus ended the sermon on the mountainside: "Listen to what I have taught you about God. If you do what I have taught—to trust God and treat people the way you want to be treated—you will be like the wise builder who built his house on a rock. When the rain came, the house on the rock stayed standing.

? How have you followed Jesus' teachings?

"If you do not do what I have taught, you will be like the foolish builder who built his house on sand. When the rain came, the house on the sand was destroyed."

The crowd was amazed by Jesus' teachings.

The Man in the Synagogue
Matthew 12:9-14

Jesus and his friends went to the synagogue—a place where Jewish people worshipped God. A man with a hurt hand was there.

The leaders at the synagogue wanted to get Jesus in trouble, so they asked him a question about God's rules.

"Do God's rules allow a person to heal on the day of rest?"

Jesus answered, "If your sheep fell into a pit on the day of rest, wouldn't you get the sheep out of the pit? People are more important than sheep. God's rules say to do what is good on the day of rest."

Jesus said to the man with the hurt hand, "Give me your hand." The man stretched out his hand, and his hand was healed.

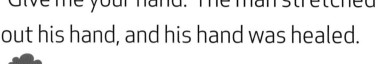

Why do you think the leaders in the synagogue wanted to get Jesus in trouble?

Jesus and the Children
Matthew 19:13-15

Some people brought their children to see Jesus. They wanted Jesus to bless their children.

The disciples were not happy. They did not want the people to bring their children to Jesus. "Don't bother Jesus!" the disciples said.

Jesus said to the disciples, "Allow the children to come to me. Don't forbid them.

"God's kingdom belongs to people like these children. You must be like these children to be a part of God's kingdom." Jesus called the children to him. He took the children in his arms and hugged them.

Why do you think the disciples tried to keep the children from Jesus?

Hosanna!
Matthew 21:1-11

Jesus and his friends, the disciples, were getting close to the city of Jerusalem. Jesus asked two of the disciples to get a donkey colt and bring it back for him to ride.

The two disciples found the donkey and brought it back to Jesus. The disciples placed their clothes on the donkey's back and placed Jesus on the donkey.

A large crowd met Jesus and the disciples at the city gate of Jerusalem. The people spread their clothes on the road. Others cut palm branches off of trees and laid them down on the road. The crowd around Jesus shouted praises, saying, "Hosanna! Blessings! Hosanna! Blessings!"

When Jesus entered Jerusalem, the whole city was excited. "Who is this?" the people in the city asked.

The crowd told the people, "This is the prophet Jesus."

? How do you think the crowd felt when they saw Jesus?

At the Last Supper
Matthew 26:17-30

Jesus' disciples asked Jesus where he wanted them to make the Passover meal.

Jesus said, "Go into the city and find a man. Tell him that my time is near and that we are going to celebrate Passover at his house." The disciples did just what they were told.

That evening Jesus and the disciples shared the Passover meal together. While they were eating, Jesus said, "One of you will let me down."

All of the disciples were sad and asked Jesus if they were the one to betray Jesus. But Jesus knew that it would be Judas.

While they ate, Jesus took the bread, blessed it, broke it, and gave it to his disciples. He said, "Take and eat. This is my body." Jesus took the cup, gave thanks, and gave it to the disciples, saying, "Drink. This is the cup of the new covenant."

After the meal, Jesus and the disciples sang songs of praise, then they walked to the Mount of Olives.

? **Have you ever had a special meal with your friends?**

In the Garden
Matthew 26:31-58

When Jesus and his friends, the disciples, got to the Mount of Olives, Jesus looked at Peter, one of his best friends. Jesus said, "Peter, before the rooster crows tonight, you will tell people you don't know me three times."

Peter was shocked, "I would never deny knowing you, Jesus!"

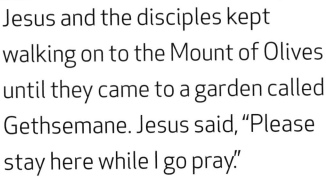

Jesus and the disciples kept walking on to the Mount of Olives until they came to a garden called Gethsemane. Jesus said, "Please stay here while I go pray."

Jesus, Peter, and Zebedee's two sons walked further in. Jesus began to feel sad and worried.

Jesus said to his three friends, "I am very sad. It is as if I am dying. Please stay here while I pray. Keep watch."

Jesus walked a little farther into the garden. He fell on his face and prayed, "Father, please take away my pain if you can. If you can't, I will do what you want and not what I want."

Jesus walked back to his friends. They were asleep! Jesus said to Peter, "Couldn't you stay awake while I prayed? Stay awake while I pray some more."

Jesus went to pray again, saying, "Father, please take away my pain if you can. Let it be what you want."

Again, Jesus walked back to his friends to find them asleep, so he went back to praying.

Jesus went to pray again, saying, "Father, please take away my pain if you can."

Then he came back to his disciples and said, "Will you sleep all night? It's time for my arrest. Get up. My betrayer is here."

Judas and a crowd of people walked toward Jesus. Judas kissed Jesus on the cheek. The crowd arrested Jesus, and the disciples ran away.

The crowd took Jesus to the high priest. Peter sneaked along, following Jesus to the courtyard of the high priest, Caiaphas.

Jesus was scared, so he prayed to God to help him. What do you do when you feel scared?

Cock-a-doodle-doo!
Matthew 26:69-75

Peter sat in the courtyard while the leaders of the temple and the Council questioned Jesus about his ministry.

A servant woman came up to Peter and said, "You were with Jesus."

Peter said, "No, I wasn't!" to the woman and to everyone in the courtyard. "You don't know what you are talking about."

Peter walked toward the gate of the courtyard. Another woman saw Peter and said, "This man was with Jesus!"

Peter looked at her and said, "I do not know that man."

Peter stood there a while longer. The people standing there said to Peter, "You must be one of Jesus' friends. The way you talk gives you away."

Then Peter cursed and swore, "I don't know the man!" At that very moment, the rooster crowed, "Cock-a-doodle-doo!"

Peter remembered what Jesus had said, "You will tell people you don't know me three times before the rooster crows."

Peter ran out of the courtyard and cried.

Peter loved Jesus. They were very good friends. Why do you think Peter told people he wasn't friends with Jesus?

Alleluia!
Matthew 28:1-10

Three days after Jesus died, Mary Magdalene and Mary went to the tomb where Jesus was buried. Suddenly, a strong earthquake shook the ground, and the women saw an angel from heaven.

The angel rolled the large stone away from the entrance to the tomb and sat on it.

The angel said to the women, "Don't be afraid! I know you are looking for Jesus, but he isn't here! Jesus is alive!"

The angel said, "I have come to tell you to go to Jesus' disciples and tell them that Jesus has risen to life." The women were excited, scared, and happy to hear the angel.

How do you think Mary Magdalene and Mary felt?

The women started running down the garden path to tell the disciples.

Suddenly, the women ran into Jesus. The women kneeled down to worship Jesus.

Jesus said to the women, "Do not be afraid. Go to my disciples and tell them to meet me in Galilee."

The Great Commission
Matthew 28:16-20

The disciples went to a mountain in Galilee to wait for Jesus. Mary Magdalene and Mary told the disciples that Jesus was alive. When Jesus appeared to the disciples, they saw him and worshipped him. Jesus said, "God has given me power over everything in heaven and earth."

Jesus gave the disciples instructions to share the good news about him with the world. Jesus said, "Go to all people and teach them about me. Baptize them. Teach them to love one another and to do all of the other things I have taught you to do. I will be with you always, wherever you go, for all time."

What is your favorite Jesus story? Tell someone the story!

Mark

The Book of Mark is an action-packed summary of the things Jesus said and did, beginning with Jesus' baptism by John the Baptizer and ending with Jesus' resurrection. This book helps people learn important truths about Jesus.

Tips for
Adults

The Book of Mark doesn't say anything about Jesus' birth, instead, it jumps right in to the ministry of Jesus' life. The Book of Mark was the first Gospel book written and was used as a source to write the Books of Matthew and Luke. Mark is the shortest of the Gospels, and highlights the healings and miracles Jesus performed.

A Voice in the Wilderness
Mark 1:9-11

Jesus traveled from his home in Nazareth to the place where John the Baptizer was baptizing people in the Jordan River. John baptized Jesus in the river.

When Jesus came up out of the water, Jesus saw heaven open and the Spirit, like a dove, came down on him. There was a voice from heaven that said, "You are my Son. I love you. You make me happy."

Who do you love?
What makes you happy?

The Four Friends
Mark 2:1-12

Jesus went back to Capernaum. People heard that he was there and came to his home. There were so many people at the house that there was not space for even one more person!

Jesus was teaching the people when four friends arrived carrying their friend who was paralyzed to Jesus on a mat. The friends could not carry him through the crowd.

The four friends did not give up!
They carried the man who was
paralyzed to the roof. They tore
through the roof of the home and
lowered their friend on his mat to
Jesus.

How do you think the people felt in this story? Have you ever helped a friend?

Jesus saw their faith and said, "You are forgiven! Get up and walk."

Right away, the man picked up his mat and walked out in front of the crowd. Everyone was amazed. They praised God!

Jesus Calms the Storm
Mark 4:35-41

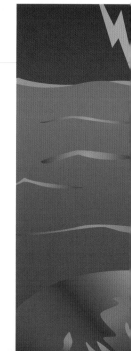

Jesus had been teaching the crowds. At the end of the day, Jesus said to the disciples, his friends, "Let's go across to the other side of the lake." They left the crowd and took a boat out into the water.

Big, strong winds began blowing the water against and into the boat! The disciples were scared, but Jesus was asleep in the back of the boat.

The disciples woke Jesus up and said, "Teacher, don't you care that we are drowning?"

Jesus got up and told the wind to be silent and still. The wind settled down, and everything was calm.

Have you ever been in a storm? What was that like?

Jesus asked the disciples, "Why are you afraid? Don't you have faith yet?"

The disciples were filled with wonder because of what Jesus had done. They looked at each other and said, "Who is this man? The wind and the sea obey him."

Jairus's Daughter
Mark 5:21-24, 35-43

When Jesus arrived at the lakeshore, a crowd of people were waiting for him. Everyone crowded around Jesus.

Jairus, an important leader, came rushing up to Jesus. He fell down at Jesus' feet. "Jesus!" cried Jairus. "My daughter is really sick. Please come make her better."

Jesus and his disciples followed Jairus to his house. While they were walking, some of Jairus's friends stopped them. Jesus and Jairus stopped walking to listen to Jairus's friends. "Your daughter is dead," said the friends. "Jesus doesn't need to come."

But Jesus shook his head. "No," said Jesus. "Don't be afraid. Keep trusting."

Jesus took two of his helpers and went to Jairus's daughter. She was lying on a bed. Her mother stood beside the bed, crying. "Why are you crying?" asked Jesus. "The child is not dead. She is only sleeping."

Who takes care of you when you are sick?

Then Jesus took the girl's hand. "Little girl," Jesus said, "get up!" And the little girl got up and began to walk around!

Go Two by Two
Mark 6:7-13

Jesus called his twelve friends and said, "I want you to go out healing and preaching, go two by two. Take nothing with you on your trip—you may only take a walking stick. Don't take bread or bags or money in your belts. You may wear sandals, but don't wear two shirts."

What do you pack when you go on a trip?

Then Jesus told his friends how to behave. Jesus said, "Choose a house where you are welcome to stay. Stay in that house until you leave that place. If you aren't welcomed, leave that town and shake the dust off your shoes. Pray for people, heal them, and make them well."

Bartimaeus Shouts to Jesus
Mark 10:46-52

Jesus and his crowd of followers had traveled to Jericho and were on their way out of town when they noticed a man named Bartimaeus sitting beside the road. Bartimaeus was blind, so he could not see. Bartimaeus was begging for someone to help him. When Bartimaeus heard that Jesus was there, he began to shout, "Jesus! Please help me!"

The crowd around Bartimaeus told him to be quiet, but he just shouted louder, "Jesus! Please help me!"

Jesus heard Bartimaeus and told Bartimaeus to come to him. Bartimaeus jumped up and came to Jesus.

Jesus asked Bartimaeus what Jesus could do for him. The blind man said, "Teacher, I want to see!"

Jesus said, "Go! Your faith has healed you!" At once, Bartimaeus was able to see and he followed Jesus.

What do you think the crowd was thinking as they watched what happened?

People Welcome Jesus
Mark 11:1-11

Jesus and his friends were walking to Jerusalem. As they passed a small town, Jesus stopped. "Go on into that town," Jesus said to two of his friends. "When you get there, you will see a donkey. Bring the donkey to me. I will ride it into the city. If anyone asks you why you are taking the donkey, tell them that Jesus needs it and he will send it back soon."

So the two friends went into the small town to find the donkey. Then they brought the donkey to Jesus.

The friends took off their coats and laid the coats across the donkey's back. Jesus sat on the donkey and started riding into the city.

When the people in the city heard that Jesus was coming, they hurried to see him. Some people spread their coats on the ground. Some people waved palm branches as they followed behind Jesus and the donkey. Many people shouted, "Hosanna! Hosanna!"

The people celebrated Jesus by waving palms, laying their coats down on the road, and shouting praises. How can you celebrate Jesus?

Jesus Breaks the Bread
Mark 14:12-26

On the first day of the Festival of Unleavened Bread, Jesus' disciples asked him where they should prepare the Passover meal. Jesus told two of the disciples what to do, "Go into the city of Jerusalem. A man carrying a water jar will meet you. Follow him.

"When he goes into a house, tell the owner that the Teacher and his disciples will eat there in his guestroom. That's where you should prepare the Passover meal."

The disciples did just what Jesus said, and they prepared the Passover meal.

That night, Jesus and his twelve friends arrived for the meal.

During the Passover meal, Jesus took bread, blessed it, broke it, and gave it to his friends. Jesus said, "Take, this is my body."

Jesus took the cup, gave thanks, and gave it to them, and they all drank from it. Jesus said, "This is the cup of the new covenant."

Jesus and the disciples finished the meal, sang songs of praise, and then went out to the Mount of Olives.

How do you think Jesus felt while sharing this special meal with his friends? Have you ever had a big feast?

Luke

The Book of Luke teaches us about what Jesus did in the world. Jesus preached the good news, healed people's minds and bodies, and showed everyone he met God's big love. Luke shows us God's love for everyone in the world!

Tips for Adults

The author of Luke also wrote the Book of Acts. The author wanted to give an organized narrative account of what happened during Jesus' life and what happened with the first believers to the early Christian groups.

This book explains Jesus' mission in the world. Jesus said he came "to preach good news to the poor, to proclaim release to the prisoners and recovery of sight to the blind, to liberate the oppressed" (Luke 4:18).

Elizabeth and Zechariah
Luke 1:5-25

There was a Jewish priest named Zechariah. He was married to Elizabeth. They were both faithful to God.

Elizabeth and Zechariah wanted to be parents, but they had gotten old. They didn't think they would ever get to have a baby.

One day Zechariah
was working in the Temple.
He went into the sanctuary to burn
incense. An angel appeared! Zechariah
was afraid. The angel said, "Don't be
afraid, Zechariah! God has heard your
prayers. Elizabeth will have a baby boy."

"You must name him John. He will serve God and help people get ready for the coming Savior."

Zechariah didn't believe the angel because it didn't make sense. He and Elizabeth were too old! "Because you don't believe, Zechariah, you will not be able to talk until John is born."

Zechariah returned home. Elizabeth was pregnant!

What a great blessing! What are some blessings you are happy about?

Gabriel's Message
Luke 1:26-38

Mary lived long ago in the little town of Nazareth. Mary was engaged to be married to Joseph, a carpenter whose family lived in Bethlehem. Mary loved God and did all of the things a young woman was supposed to do.

One day Mary heard a voice. Looking up, she saw an angel standing nearby. At first Mary was frightened!

But the angel Gabriel spoke to her, saying, "Don't be afraid, Mary. God is pleased with you."

Gabriel said, "I have come to tell you good news! God is going to send you a baby boy. You will name him Jesus. He is God's own dear Son, and he is God's greatest gift to the world. He will show everyone how to help one another and how to be happy together."

Mary listened closely to the angel, and her heart was filled with happiness. "I am a servant of God. I will do what God wants me to do," Mary told the angel Gabriel.

? How do you think Mary felt in this story?
Do you say yes when God asks you to do big things like Mary?

Mary Visits Elizabeth
Luke 1:39-66

The angel Gabriel had brought good news to Mary—she was going to have a baby boy! Her relative, Elizabeth, was also pregnant. Mary wanted to share the good news about her pregnancy with Elizabeth, so she hurried from her house to Elizabeth's house.

"Elizabeth! Elizabeth! I have good news to share with you!" shouted Mary.

"Wow!" exclaimed Elizabeth. "Mary, as soon as I heard your greeting, my baby leaped for joy! You are very blessed. You are pregnant with God's Son!"

"With all of my heart, I praise God!" sang Mary.

? Mary praised God with singing. How do you like to praise God?

Jesus Is Born
Luke 2:1-7

Mary and Joseph had traveled a long way from Nazareth to Bethlehem. The emperor wanted everyone to go to their hometowns to be counted.

Joseph was from Bethlehem, so he and Mary had to go to Bethlehem. It had been a hard trip—Mary was going to have her baby very soon!

Bethlehem was very crowded and busy. There was no room for Mary and Joseph in the guestroom.

That special night, baby Jesus was born. Mary wrapped him in cloth and laid him in a manger.

This is Jesus' birth story. What is your birth story?

Joyous News
Luke 2:8-20

In the fields around Bethlehem, shepherds were watching their sheep.

That night an angel appeared to the shepherds. The angel said, "Do not be afraid. Today in Bethlehem a baby was born for everyone! The baby is God's Son. The baby's name is Jesus! You will find him lying in a manger."

The shepherds said, "Let's go to Bethlehem and see this special baby!"

The shepherds found Mary and Joseph and baby Jesus. They told everyone they saw about the new baby.

The shepherds praised God for letting them see the special baby Jesus.

? **How do you think the shepherds felt that night?**

Simeon and Anna
Luke 2:25-31

It was a very special day for baby Jesus. Joseph and Mary were taking Jesus to the Temple for the first time. Jesus was going to be dedicated to God at the Temple.

Simeon watched as the young family came inside God's Temple. Simeon was very old and loved God very much.

He walked over to Mary and Joseph, and asked if he could hold Jesus. "This is all I have lived for," said Simeon. "A long time ago, God promised me that I would live long enough to see the Messiah, and here he is!" Simeon was so happy, he sang a song of praise and thanksgiving to God.

Just then, an old woman approached
the group gathered around baby Jesus.
Her name was Anna. Anna was an old
prophetess. She saw Jesus' face and
declared that Jesus was the Messiah to
all who could hear. She praised God for
the Messiah, just like Simeon.

How do you like to praise
God when good things
happen?

Talk With the Teachers

Luke 2:39-52

When Jesus was growing up, his parents, Mary and Joseph, traveled to the city of Jerusalem every year to celebrate the holiday of Passover.

When Jesus was twelve years old, Mary and Joseph traveled to Jerusalem as usual.

When the holiday was over, Mary and Joseph started traveling back home when they noticed that Jesus was not with them.

Mary and Joseph looked for Jesus among all their friends and family, but Mary and Joseph could not find their son.

After three days of looking for Jesus, Mary and Joseph finally found him. Jesus was in the Temple talking to the church leaders. Jesus understood so much about God that the church leaders were amazed!

When Mary and Joseph found Jesus, Mary said to Jesus, "Son, why have you done this to us? We have been worried about you! We have been looking for you!"

Jesus did not understand what his mother was asking. Jesus asked Mary, "Didn't you know that I would be in the Temple, in the house of God, my Father?"

Mary and Joseph did not understand what Jesus meant, but Mary remembered everything Jesus had said, and she kept those memories in her heart.

Jesus returned to Nazareth with Mary and Joseph, and Jesus obeyed them. Jesus grew up and became wise. God was pleased with Jesus, and so were people!

What do you think Jesus told the teachers at the Temple?

Jesus Is Baptized
Luke 3:1-22

The man standing in the river said, "Come into the water and be baptized."

The man was John the Baptizer. Many people came to be baptized and listen to John teach about God.

"Change your hearts and lives," said John. "Show everyone that you want to live the way God wants you to live."

One by one, people walked into the river. They felt the cool water flowing around them. When John baptized them with this cool water, they felt God's love.

One day Jesus came to the river. John baptized Jesus with the cool water of the river.

As Jesus was baptized, a dove came flying down from the sky. Jesus saw the dove and heard God's voice saying, "You are my Son, whom I dearly love."

We are a part of God's family too! How does it make you feel to know that God dearly loves you?

Jesus Chooses
Luke 4:1-13

After Jesus was baptized, he went into the wilderness for forty days of fasting. After forty days of not eating, Jesus was very hungry.

The tempter came to talk to Jesus.

"See these rocks on the ground," said the tempter. "Go ahead and turn those rocks into bread. Then you can eat. I know you're hungry."

But Jesus said to the tempter, "It is written in the Scriptures that people don't live only by bread."

The tempter decided to try a second time.

He took Jesus to the top of the mountain.

"Look at all the kingdoms of the world! If you will worship me instead of God, I will let you be king over the whole world."

But Jesus said to the tempter, "It is written in the Scriptures that we are to worship and serve God, no one else."

? Have you ever been tempted to make a bad choice?

The tempter decided to try a third time. He took Jesus to the top of the Temple of God.

"Go ahead and jump down from the Temple. You know you won't get hurt because you are God's Son."

But Jesus said to the tempter, "It is written in the Scriptures that we should not test God."

So the tempter gave up and left. Jesus was once again alone in the wilderness, thinking about God and what God wanted him to do.

Jesus Brings Good News
Luke 4:14-30

Jesus traveled back to his hometown, Nazareth. It was the sabbath day and time to worship God, so Jesus went to the synagogue. At the synagogue, Jesus read the scroll with the words of the prophet Isaiah written on it.

Jesus opened the scroll and read, "God's Spirit is on me. God has chosen me to bring good news to the poor, the prisoners, the blind, and those who are mistreated. God's blessing has come." Jesus rolled up the scroll.

This story in Luke is very important. It sets up the rest of Luke's book. Jesus will do each of these things in the upcoming stories. It also outlines what we are called to do as Christians.

Everyone was watching him. He said, "Those words were written hundreds of years ago. Today, those words have come true." The people were amazed by Jesus.

Jesus teaches us how to love and care for one another. How did you care for another today?

"He's Joseph's son, isn't he?" whispered one of the people.

Jesus told the people that he would not be welcome in his hometown, and that he planned to be like the prophets Elijah and Elisha who healed people even if they were not Israelites.

This made the people angry! They chased Jesus toward a cliff, but Jesus walked through the crowd and continued on his way.

Jesus Heals
Luke 4:38-44

Jesus walked from the city of Nazareth, his hometown, to the city of Capernaum. While he was in the city, he taught the people about God's love.

Then Jesus went with Peter to Peter's home. Peter's mother-in-law was sick. She had a high fever.

Jesus bent over Peter's mother-in-law and spoke to her. Immediately, the fever went away.

Peter's mother-in-law felt so much better that she got up and served everyone.

At the end of the day, many people brought their family and friends who were sick to Jesus. Jesus touched them and healed them.

Then Jesus went to another city to teach the people about God's love.

Peter's mother-in-law served everyone after being healed by Jesus. Why do you think she did that?

Jesus Calls Levi
Luke 5:27-32

Jesus saw a tax collector named Levi sitting at a desk by the Sea of Galilee. Jesus went to Levi and said, "Follow me." Levi got up from his desk and followed Jesus. Levi said to Jesus, "Come, eat at my house. I want to throw a feast for you."

Jesus sat down to eat with Levi and his friends. Levi's friends were tax collectors. People did not like tax collectors because tax collectors took more money than they should from people. Sometimes tax collectors were not honest. Sometimes tax collectors cheated and stole from people.

The leaders grumbled to Jesus. The leaders asked, "Why do you sit down and eat with people who do bad things?"

Jesus said, "I didn't come to leave out people who make mistakes, but to include them."

? Have you ever been left out before? How did that make you feel? How do you think Levi felt being included in Jesus' group of friends?

The Two Debtors
Luke 7:41-43

Jesus was eating with a Pharisee named Simon. While he was eating, a woman cleaned Jesus' feet with tears, her hair, and very expensive perfumed oil. Simon was unhappy that Jesus let the woman do this to his feet.

Jesus chose to tell Simon a story to help Simon better understand why Jesus let the woman clean his feet.

Jesus said, "Two people owed a money-lender money. One person owed enough money to pay five hundred people for a day's work. The other person owed enough money to pay fifty people for a day's work. They could not pay back the money. The lender didn't make them pay any of the money back. Who do you think was the most thankful?"

Simon answered, "The one who owed the most money."

Who do you think was the most thankful? Is Simon right?

Women Follow Jesus
Luke 8:1-3

Jesus traveled to many towns. Everywhere Jesus went, he told people about God's love.

Jesus traveled with twelve friends. Jesus' twelve friends helped Jesus tell people about God's love.

How can you help share Jesus' love like the women?

There were also some women who helped Jesus tell people about God's love. The women's names were Mary Magdalene, Joanna, and Susanna. The twelve friends, and the women, were Jesus' helpers.

The Sower
Luke 8:4-15

Jesus traveled from city to city,
teaching crowds of people by telling
them stories. Jesus told the crowd this
story:

A farmer scattered seeds. Some of
the seeds fell on the path where it was
crushed and eaten by birds.

Some of the seeds fell on rocks, but as
the seeds grew, the plants dried up.

Some of the seeds fell near thorny plants.
When the seeds grew into plants, the
thorny plants choked the seeds.
Some of the seeds landed on good soil.
When the seeds grew, they made one
hundred times more grain than was
scattered.

Jesus then said, "Everyone should pay attention to this story."

Jesus explained the story, "The seed is God's story. The seeds that fell on the path represent people who hear God's story, but it doesn't mean anything to them. The seeds that fell on the rocks represent people who hear God's story, believe it for a little while, but forget it."

Jesus continued, "The seeds that fell among the thorny plants represent the people who hear God's story, but let fear and worries and anxiety keep them from living the way God wants them to. The seeds that fell on good soil represent people who hear God's story and live the way God wants them to."

What do you think is the most important part of this story?

The Good Samaritan

Luke 10:25-37

A legal expert asked Jesus, "What do I need to do to have eternal life?"

Jesus answered him with a question, "What does the Law say?"

The legal expert quoted God's Law, "You must love the Lord your God with all your heart, with all your being, with all your

strength, and with all your mind, and love your neighbor as yourself."

Jesus said, "That's right. Do this and you will live."

But the legal expert wanted to trick Jesus, so he asked, "Who is my neighbor?"

To answer his question, Jesus told a story:

There was a man traveling from Jerusalem to Jericho. While he was walking the dangerous road, he was beaten up really badly by thieves and left on the side of the road. He was nearly dead.

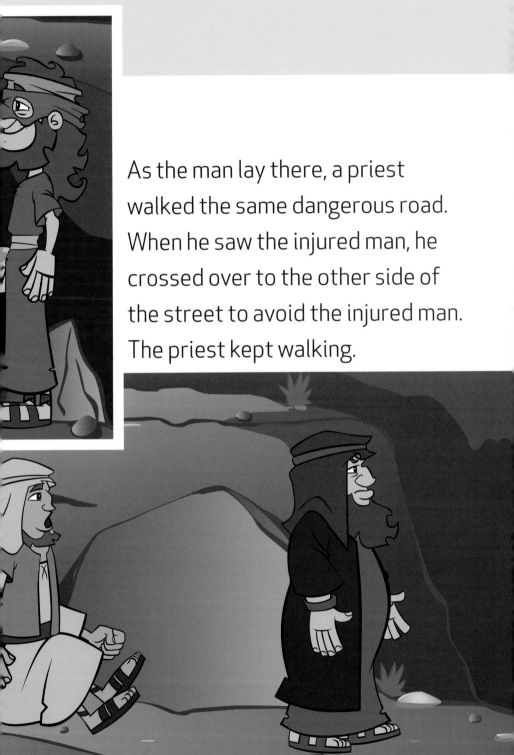

As the man lay there, a priest walked the same dangerous road. When he saw the injured man, he crossed over to the other side of the street to avoid the injured man. The priest kept walking.

A Levite, a person who worked in a synagogue, also was walking down this dangerous road. When he saw the injured man, he crossed over to the other side of the street to avoid the injured man.

There was also a Samaritan walking this dangerous road. We all know that Samaritans are enemies of the Jewish people.

But when the Samaritan saw the injured man, he felt compassion. He knew it was right to help the injured man. The Samaritan bandaged the man's wounds, placed the man on his donkey, and took him to an inn to care for him.

Jesus asked the listeners, "What do you think? Which one of these three people was a neighbor to the injured man?"

The legal expert answered, "The one who showed care."

Jesus teaches us to love our enemies. How do we show love to all people?

Mary and Martha

Luke 10:38-42

Jesus and his disciples were traveling, and they needed a place to rest. Jesus' friends, Mary and Martha, invited Jesus to stay with them. When Jesus arrived, Mary sat at his feet to listen to him. Martha served everyone.

Martha was tired and thought it was unfair when she saw that Mary was sitting at Jesus' feet instead of helping.

"Jesus, it's not fair that Mary is not helping. Tell her to help me!" said Martha.

"Martha, what Mary has been doing is important," Jesus said. "Mary has chosen to be close to me and to learn about God. It is important to be close to me and to learn about God."

How do you think Martha felt in this story? How do you think Mary felt? How do you think Jesus felt?

The Mustard Seed & the Yeast
Luke 13:18-21

esus asked, "What is God's kingdom like? What can I compare God's kingdom to? God's kingdom is like a tiny mustard seed that someone planted in a garden. The mustard seed grew and grew, and became a tree. It got so big that birds nested in its branches."

Jesus continued, "God's kingdom is like yeast that a woman hid in flour. The yeast made all of the flour grow into raised dough."

What do you think God's kingdom is like?

The Stories of the Lost
Luke 15:3-10

Jesus was teaching a big crowd of people by telling stories called parables. He told them this parable: Pretend that you had one hundred sheep, and you lost one. Wouldn't you realize you lost the sheep and leave the ninety-nine sheep to find the one lost sheep?

When you find the lost sheep, you would call together all of your friends and neighbors, and have a party to celebrate the found sheep because your flock is whole again.

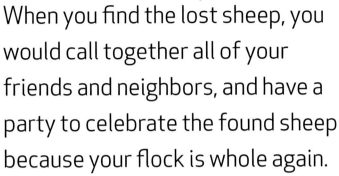

Jesus continued teaching by telling another parable:

What woman, if she owns ten silver coins and loses one, realizing she has lost the coin, won't light a lamp and look for the lost coin carefully until she finds it?

When she finds the lost coin, she would call her friends and neighbors, and have a celebration for the found coin because her group of coins is whole again.

Have you ever lost something or someone? What did you do?

The Forgiving Father
Luke 15:11-32

esus was teaching a big crowd of people by telling stories called parables. He told them this parable: There was a man with two sons. The younger son said to his father, "Give me my share of the inheritance." The father divided all of the things he owned and all of his money between the older son and the younger son.

The younger son took all of the things his father gave him, took a trip, and wasted all of the money he had been given.

The place he traveled to didn't have much food. The younger son was in need of food. He took a job to feed pigs. He was so hungry, he wanted to eat the food for the pigs.

The younger son thought about home. Even the hired hands on his dad's land were fed well. He decided to go home and see if his father would hire him to work.

While the younger son was still a ways off, the father saw him and he was filled with love for his son. The father ran to meet his son, hugged him, and kissed him.

The younger son said, "Father, I made a bad choice. I don't deserve to be your son."

But the father threw a big party and served the best food to celebrate that his younger son had come home.

The older brother found out what was going on, and he was angry! He did not want to celebrate his brother's return home. His father came out to him and begged him to come to the party.

The older son said, "I have worked for you and have never disobeyed you. You have

never thrown a party for me, but you are throwing a party for my brother who has disobeyed you!"

The father said, "Son, you are always with me and everything I have is yours. Celebrating your brother's return does not change my love for you."

How do you think the older brother felt in this story?

Ten Lepers

Luke 17:11-19

Jesus was walking to Jerusalem, and on the way he saw ten men. The men were very sick. The men had a skin sickness called leprosy. The men were not allowed to be around anyone but each other.

The men saw Jesus, and they yelled out to him, "Jesus, please heal us! We are ten very sick men!"

Jesus saw the ten men. Jesus said, "Go show yourselves to the priests."

The ten men turned around and started walking to see the priests, but on the way, something happened. The ten men were healed! All the spots on their skin went away!

One of the men who was healed turned around and ran back to Jesus. The man said, "Thank you, Jesus, for healing me!"

Jesus asked, "Why did only one of you return? Weren't ten men healed?" Jesus said to the man, "Your faith has made you well."

? How do you think the ten men felt when they were sick? How do you think the ten men felt when they were healed?

Patience
Luke 18:1-8

Jesus taught the people through storytelling. One story he told was about a judge who did not fear God or respect people. A widow, a woman whose husband had died, kept coming to this judge asking for justice. The judge kept refusing.

Finally, the judge said that he would give the woman justice so she would stop bothering him. Jesus said, "If this judge would give the woman what she needed, won't God provide justice for his chosen people?"

How does it feel when things are not fair? How can you be like the widow who asked for things to be made fair?

The Pharisee & the Tax Collecto
Luke 18:9-14

J esus taught the crowd by telling this story:

Two men went to the temple to pray to God. One man was a Pharisee, a church leader. The other man was a tax collector. No one liked tax collectors.

The Pharisee stood up and spoke his prayer out loud, "Dear God, thank you for who I am. I am so good! I am not a bad person. I do not lie or steal or cheat. I am not like this tax collector! I do everything right. I say all of my prayers. I share my money with the poor. I never break your rules!"

The tax collector was ashamed of himself. He stood away from the people in the temple, with his eyes looking down at the floor. "Dear God," the tax collector prayed, "I am sorry for all of the wrong choices I have made. I am not perfect. Please forgive me."

What is your favorite way to pray?

The tax collector beat his chest and cried out loud.

Jesus finished his story for the people: "God loves us all. No one is better than anyone else."

Zacchaeus

Luke 19:1-10

esus was walking through the town of Jericho. A tax collector named Zacchaeus was there in Jericho and wanted to see Jesus walk by. He was too short to see over the crowd, so he ran ahead and climbed a tree.

When Jesus got to the tree Zacchaeus had climbed, Jesus looked up and said, "Zacchaeus, come down. I must stay at your home today."

Zacchaeus immediately climbed down the tree, happy to welcome Jesus to his home.

The crowd was very unhappy with Jesus for being a guest of a tax collector. They grumbled because tax collectors were known for being unfair.

Zaccheus heard what the crowd was saying. He looked at Jesus and made this promise, "Lord, I will give half of everything I own to the poor. And if I have

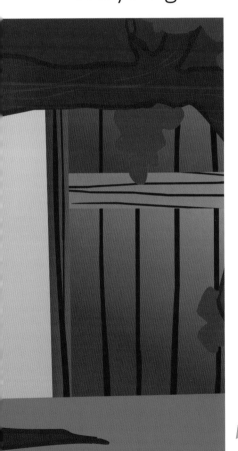

cheated anyone, I will repay them four times what I have taken."

Jesus knew Zaccheus meant what he said. Jesus said, "Zaccheus, today you have been saved."

Have you ever cheated? How did that make you feel? How do you think Zaccheus felt when he decided to be fair?

The Ten Talents
Luke 19:11-26

Jesus taught the people in Jericho about earthly kingdoms through telling a story called a parable.

He told this story, "There was a man born into a family of power. He decided to go to a distant land to get his own kingdom.

"We know that nothing good happens in a distant land."

Jesus continued, "Before the man left, he gave ten servants four months' worth of money. He told the servants to make him more money while he was gone. The man left the servants, and when he returned, he called them all back to him."

The people listened to Jesus some more, "The first servant made the king ten times more money, so the king gave the servant ten cities. The second servant made five times more money, so the king gave the servant five cities. The third servant came forward, but hadn't made any more money. The king was angry and greedy."

Jesus told the people this story because God's kingdom would be nothing like this man's kingdom.

How do you think God's kingdom is different than this man's kingdom?

Jesus Enters Jerusalem
Luke 19:28-40

Jesus gave two disciples a job. He said, "Go into the village. You will find a colt there that no one has ridden. Bring the colt here."

The disciples did what Jesus told them to do and brought the colt to Jesus.

The disciples put their clothes on the colt's back and helped Jesus onto the colt. As Jesus rode along, the disciples spread their clothes on the road. The whole crowd rejoiced when they saw Jesus, saying, "Blessings! Peace!"

Some of the Pharisees told Jesus to make the disciples stop rejoicing. Jesus answered them, "If they didn't rejoice, stones would shout praises!"

What do you think the stones would say?

The Widow's Coins
Luke 21:1-4

Jesus and the disciples were at the temple. He saw rich people putting their money gifts into the offering box. Jesus also saw a poor widow throw in two small copper coins worth a penny.

Jesus said to his disciples, "We are supposed to care for the widows. Instead, she must give all that she has to the temple. I promise you she has given more than all of the others because she has given everything she has."

Are there people like the widow in your community you could help care for?

Jesus Celebrates Passover
Luke 22:7-20

Jesus and his friends had traveled to Jerusalem to celebrate the Passover feast. Jesus sent Peter and John ahead of the group, saying, "Peter and John, please go and prepare the Passover meal for us so we can eat together."

Peter and John went ahead of the group and prepared the meal.

When the time came for the meal, Jesus and his friends sat at the table that Peter and John had prepared. Jesus told his disciples, "I have really wanted to eat this Passover meal with you."

Then Jesus held the cup and gave thanks to God. "Take this cup and share it," said Jesus to his disciples. Then Jesus picked up a loaf of bread. He broke the bread, blessed it, and gave it to them. "Do this in remembrance of me," said Jesus to his disciples.

After supper, Jesus said, "This cup is the new promise, the new covenant. Drink it and remember me."

The disciples were happy to share this special meal with Jesus, but they did not understand what was about to happen.

What do you remember about Jesus?

The Tomb Is Empty
Luke 24:1-12

Mary Magdalene, Joanna, Mary the mother of James, and the other women were very sad. Jesus had been killed on a cross. They wanted to prepare his body, so very early on Sunday morning, the women went to Jesus' tomb right outside of the gates in Jerusalem.

But when the women got to Jesus' tomb, they found the stone rolled away. When they went inside of the tomb, they didn't find Jesus' body. They didn't know what to think about this.

Suddenly, two angels appeared.
The women were afraid. The angels
said, "Why are you looking for Jesus
here? He isn't here. He has risen!"

The women ran to the disciples and
told them what had happened at
Jesus' tomb.

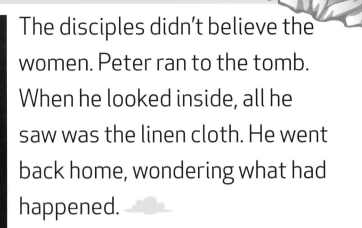

The disciples didn't believe the women. Peter ran to the tomb. When he looked inside, all he saw was the linen cloth. He went back home, wondering what had happened.

? How do you think the women felt in the story?

The Road to Emmaus

Luke 24:13-35

On Sunday, Cleopas and his friend were walking from Jerusalem to Emmaus. They were talking about what had happened in Jerusalem. As they walked, a stranger began walking with them. "What are you talking about?" asked the stranger.

Cleopas said sadly, "We were talking about Jesus. Jesus was a man of God. He was killed three days ago."

Cleopas continued, "This morning the women went to Jesus' tomb, but Jesus was not there. Angels told them that Jesus is alive!

"Peter went to the tomb, and he did not find Jesus either."

The stranger asked, "Why can't you believe what the prophets said?" The stranger began explaining all of the things that were written by the prophets.

When they got to Emmaus, Cleopas and his friend invited the stranger to stay and eat with them.

When dinner was ready, they all sat down to eat. The stranger took the bread, broke it, and blessed it. Then he gave each person some bread. When the stranger did this, Cleopas and his friend recognized him. It was Jesus!

As soon as they recognized Jesus, he disappeared. The friends got up quickly and returned to Jerusalem to find the other disciples. They told the disciples, "The Lord really has risen!"

Why do you think Cleopas and his friend didn't recognize Jesus?

John

The story of Jesus in the Book of John is different from the story in any other New Testament book. The author of John tells the story of Jesus using beautiful words and pictures.

Tips for
Adults

The Book of John was probably the last of the four Gospels—Matthew, Mark, Luke, and John—written. The author is unknown, though tradition says that John, son of Zebedee, wrote the book. The Book of John focuses more on who Jesus is, the Son of God, and teaches less about God's kingdom. John teaches us that Jesus was "the Word" who was with God at the very beginning.

Change the Water
John 2:1-12

One day Jesus, his mother, and his friends went to a wedding in the town of Capernaum.

When the guests were eating and drinking, Jesus' mother said to Jesus, "There is no more wine left to drink."

Mary said to the servants, "Do whatever Jesus tells you."

Jesus said to the servants, "Go fill those six big jars with water—all the way to the top! After you have filled them, take some water and give it to the man in charge of the wedding supper."

The man in charge drank some of the water, but it had turned into wine, and it was very good!

The man in charge said to the groom, "Most of the time, the best wine is served at the beginning of the wedding supper, but you have saved the best until last."

Jesus had turned the water into wine.

How do you think Jesus' friends felt when they knew Jesus had changed water into wine?

Born Anew
John 3:1-21

Nicodemus was a Jewish leader. One night he came to talk to Jesus.

"Jesus, we know that you are a teacher from God," said Nicodemus. "You could only do miracles if God was with you. How do I see God's kingdom?"

"You must be born anew if you want to see God's kingdom," answered Jesus.

"How is it possible for a grownup to be born a second time?" asked Nicodemus. "That's impossible."

"Everyone is first born as a baby," said Jesus. "I'm talking about our spirit, the part of us that feels God's love. Our spirit must be born anew."

"How is this possible?" asked Nicodemus.

"God loved the world so much that God gave the world a special gift. That gift was God's Son," said Jesus. "Everyone who believes in God's Son will live with God forever."

How does it feel to know that God loves you?

The Woman at the Well
John 4:1-42

One day Jesus and his friends went to Samaria. Jesus was hot and tired. Jesus sat down by a well. Jesus' friends went to buy food because they were hungry.

A woman came up to the well where Jesus was sitting. Jesus started talking to the woman. Jesus said, "I know all about you, and I know that you need to follow God." The woman was very surprised.

The woman said to Jesus, "How do you know all about me?"

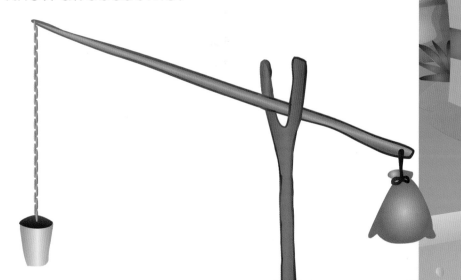

Jesus said, "I know all about you because I am the Son of God, and I know that God loves you very much, even though you have made some mistakes."

The woman ran and told others in the town about Jesus.

Many people in Samaria began to believe in Jesus because of what the woman told them. They began to follow Jesus because they believed that Jesus was the Son of God.

How do you think the woman felt when Jesus spoke to her?

The Man by the Pool

John 5:1-17

One day Jesus walked to a place where there was a pool of swirling water. Many sick people visited the pool because they thought the water would make them well.

Sitting by the pool was a man who had not been able to walk for many years.

Jesus saw the man and asked, "Do you want to get well?"

The man said, "Jesus, I want to get in the pool when the water is swirling, but I need someone to lift me in, and someone else always gets in before anyone can help me."

Jesus said, "Pick up your mat and walk!"

Immediately, the man got up! He picked up his mat and walked away from the pool.

Jesus healed the man on a sabbath
day. On sabbath days, nobody was
supposed to do any work, including
healing sick people.

When the Jewish leaders heard
that Jesus had healed the man on
the sabbath day, they became very
angry.

How do you think the man felt when he was able to get up and walk?

Jesus knew the Jewish leaders would get angry, but Jesus helped people whenever he could, even on sabbath days.

A Boy's Lunch
John 6:1-15

One sunny day, Jesus and his disciples crossed the Sea of Galilee. A huge crowd followed them. The crowd had heard about Jesus' stories and about the miracles he was performing. The crowd hoped to see the power of God through Jesus this very day.

The crowd followed Jesus and the disciples up into the mountains. Jesus looked out into the crowd and said to his friend, Philip, "There have to be over five thousand people here, and they haven't eaten anything. Where can we buy food for these people?"

Philip knew they could not afford to buy food for that many people.

Another disciple, Andrew, noticed a boy in the crowd who had five loaves of bread and two fish. Andrew brought the boy to Jesus.

"It isn't much, but this boy has some food," Andrew said to Jesus.

"If you think it will help," said the boy, "I'll be happy to share my food."

Jesus instructed the crowd to sit down. Then Jesus took the bread and fish, and said, "Dear God, thank you for our blessings." Jesus broke the bread and fish, and began passing it out to the people.

Everyone in the crowd ate until each person was full. Jesus performed a miracle!

"Pick up what is left," Jesus instructed his friends. There were twelve baskets of food left!

Jesus cares about full bellies, and so should we. How can you help others get enough food to eat?

Jesus Walks on Water
John 6:16-25

Get in the boat and go to the other side of the lake," Jesus told his friends. "I'm going up the mountain to pray."

The friends did what Jesus told them to do. They got into the boat and started sailing across the lake.

The lake was calm. There were no waves. It was nighttime. The stars were beginning to shine as Jesus' friends sailed across the lake.

Suddenly, the wind started to blow. The waves in the water were getting higher and higher.

The waves crashed against the sides of the boat. They splashed water into the boat.

The waves crashed and splashed all night.

Finally, the morning came. As the sky began to lighten, Jesus' friends looked over the crashing waves.

They saw someone walking across the waves toward their boat.

"Who is that?" the friends cried. "Is it a ghost?" Jesus' friends were afraid.

But it was not a ghost. It was Jesus! Jesus was walking across the waves to the boat.

"I want to walk on water too," said Peter. He stepped out of the boat and started walking on the waves to Jesus.

Then Peter looked down and saw the waves splashing around him. He started to sink!

"Help me, Jesus!" Peter cried.

Jesus walked across the waves, grabbed Peter's hand, and said, "Have faith!"

Peter and Jesus climbed into the boat. When they were safely in the boat, the wind stopped blowing and the waves stopped splashing.

Jesus' friends were surprised that Jesus could walk on the water.

They knew that Jesus was God's Son.

What would you have done if you were a disciple in the boat?

Mary Honors Jesus
John 12:1-8

Lazarus, Martha, and Mary hosted a dinner for Jesus and his friends, the disciples, in their home in Bethany.

While everyone was eating, Mary carried a jar filled with something very special into the room where everyone was eating. Inside the jar was three-quarters-of-a-pound of very expensive, sweet-smelling nard perfume.

Mary knelt on the floor by Jesus. Mary dumped and rubbed the entire jar of perfume onto Jesus' feet. Mary anointed Jesus' feet with the perfume. Mary slowly and tenderly wiped the perfume off Jesus' feet with her hair.

"Jesus, what are you letting her do?" asked Judas. "Can't you see how wasteful that is? That perfume cost a year's worth of wages! Shouldn't the perfume have been sold and the money given to the poor?"

Jesus spoke, "Leave Mary alone. Yes, the money could have been used for the poor, but there will always be people who will need you to help them. I will not be with you much longer."

? Why do you think Mary wanted to honor Jesus? How can you show love to Jesus?

Jesus Washes Feet
John 13:1-17

The friends watched as Jesus got up from the table and tied a towel around his waist. Then Jesus poured water into a big bowl.

What is Jesus doing? thought the friends. The friends watched as Jesus began to wash their feet.

"Jesus, what are you doing?" asked Peter. "I don't want you to wash my feet. My feet are so dirty. Besides, it's the job of a servant to wash feet. It's not your job. You are our teacher."

"Peter," said Jesus, "it is important that I wash your feet." So Peter let Jesus wash his dirty feet.

When Jesus finished washing everyone's feet, he took off the towel and put away the bowl of water. "Do you understand why I did the job of a servant and washed your feet?" asked Jesus.

"No," said Peter and his friends, shaking their heads.

"I wanted to show you God's love," said Jesus. "So even though I am your teacher, I did the job of a servant and washed your feet," said Jesus. "I want you to serve others. Helping others is one way to show God's love."

How do you think Peter felt when Jesus washed his feet?

Jesus Lives
John 20:1-18

Mary Magdalene walked to the tomb Jesus had been buried in. She was very sad. Her friend, Jesus, had been hurt and killed on a cross.

She approached the tomb. The giant stone that had been placed in front of the tomb had been rolled away. Worried something had happened to Jesus, Mary Magdalene ran to Peter and John.

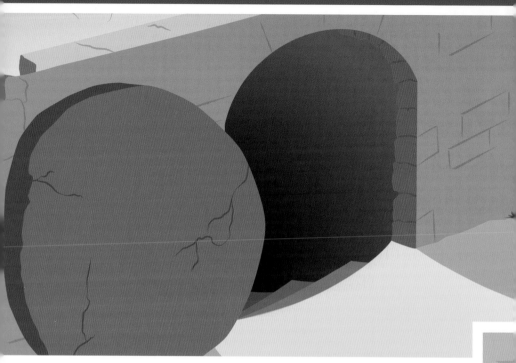

"The stone has been rolled away from the tomb! Someone must have taken Jesus!" cried Mary Magdalene to Peter and John.

Peter, John, and Mary Magdalene ran to the tomb. John got to the tomb first, looked in, and found the linens Jesus had been wrapped in laying there. Peter walked into the tomb and also saw the linens left in the tomb. They didn't quite understand what was happening. Peter and John ran back to the other disciples.

Mary Magdalene stayed behind. She stood outside of Jesus' tomb crying. A man walked up behind her. He said, "Why are you crying?" Mary Magdalene thought this man was the gardener, and she replied, "Tell me where you have put Jesus."

But the man was not a gardener. "Mary," Jesus said.

"Teacher! Jesus!" Mary Magdalene exclaimed.

"Mary, tell the disciples that I am alive," Jesus instructed.

Mary Magdalene ran through the garden all the way back to the disciples. "I have seen Jesus!" Mary Magdalene told them.

Jesus lives! How do you think Mary felt telling all of her friends that Jesus is alive?

Thomas Believes
John 20:24-31

We've seen Jesus!" said the other disciples. Thomas didn't believe what the disciples told him.

"I doubt it. Jesus has died. I would only believe that you saw Jesus if I saw Jesus with my own eyes," replied Thomas.

Eight days later, the disciples—this time, Thomas was with them—were in their hiding place again. They had all the doors locked and were sitting in the room trying to decide what to do next. All of a sudden, Jesus appeared.

"Peace be with you," said Jesus. "Thomas, don't doubt. Believe!"

"It's you, Jesus!" exclaimed Thomas.

Jesus said to Thomas, "Do you only believe because you see me? Have faith! Believe!"

Can you think of something that you believe about Jesus?

Come to Breakfast!
John 21:1-14

Peter said to his friends, "I'm going fishing; want to go with me?" They grabbed their nets and headed to the sea. They all climbed in a boat and rowed out a ways. They cast out their nets, but there were no fish. The disciples continued fishing through the night—casting out their nets and bringing them back in—but they never caught one fish.

In the morning, a man appeared on the shore. The man called out to the disciples, "If you cast your net to the other side of the boat, you will catch some fish!" The disciples weren't sure, but they threw their nets out to the other side of the boat. This time, so many fish were caught in the net, the disciples could hardly pull the net back in!

"Look, the man on the shore; it's Jesus!"
said John. Peter jumped out of the boat
and ran through the shallow water to
Jesus. The other disciples followed
Peter's lead to shore. Jesus was on the
shore, sitting by a fire.

How do you think the disciples felt seeing Jesus on the beach?

"Bring some of the fish you just caught, and we can all eat some fish and bread for breakfast," Jesus said. Jesus took the fish, said a prayer to God, and shared the fish with the disciples. Jesus took the bread, said a prayer of thanks to God, and shared the bread with the disciples.

Feed My Sheep!
John 21:15-19

When Jesus and the disciples finished eating breakfast on the beach, Jesus asked Peter a question, "Peter, do you love me?"

Peter answered, "Yes, Jesus, you know that I love you."

Jesus said to Peter, "Feed my lambs. Share God's love with everyone." Jesus asked Peter again, "Peter, do you love me?"

Peter answered, "Yes, Jesus, you know that I love you."

Jesus said to Peter, "Take care of my sheep." Jesus asked Peter again, "Peter, do you love me?"

Peter was very sad that Jesus asked him a third time if he loved Jesus. Peter answered, "Yes, Jesus, you know everything. You know that I love you. You are my best friend."

Jesus said to him, "Feed my sheep. Follow my example."

How do you think Peter felt?

Acts

The Book of Acts tells the exciting story of how the first churches formed and grew. After Jesus died and came back to life, the Holy Spirit helped the disciples to travel many places to spread the good news about Jesus.

Tips for Adults

The author of Luke also wrote the Book of Acts. Acts tells the story of how the early Christians grew together in faith and spread the good news about Jesus. Leaders like Peter and John told about Jesus, even when doing so landed them in prison.

Pentecost
Acts 2:1-41

The disciples were waiting together in a house in Jerusalem. Suddenly, a sound like a howling fierce wind filled the entire house. The disciples looked around to see what was happening.

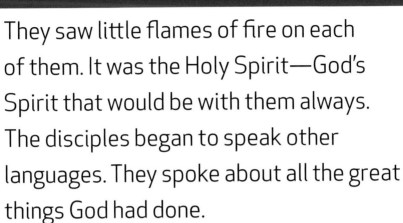

They saw little flames of fire on each of them. It was the Holy Spirit—God's Spirit that would be with them always. The disciples began to speak other languages. They spoke about all the great things God had done.

People outside the house heard the noises coming from inside the house. "What is happening?" the people wondered. Some people were confused. "What does all this mean?" they asked.

Peter spoke to the people: "God has sent the Holy Spirit to us. That is what you have seen and heard."

The people listened to Peter as he told them about Jesus. Peter encouraged the people to believe in Jesus and to be baptized. "The Holy Spirit will be given to you!" Peter told the people.

Many of the people believed Peter's words. Three thousand people were baptized and became followers of Jesus that day.

Wonder about the people in this story—how do you think they felt when this happened?

Peter and John
Acts 3:1–4:22

It was three o'clock in the afternoon. It was time for prayer in the Temple. Peter and John went to the Temple to pray.

As they were walking into the Temple, they saw a man who could not walk being carried into the Temple. He was laid down by the gate. Every day the man sat there and begged people for money.

Peter and John entered the Temple. The man saw Peter and John, and he asked them for money.

Peter said to the man who could not walk, "Look at us!"

The man who could not walk looked at Peter and John. The man thought Peter and John would give him some money.

Peter said, "I do not have money to give you, but I have a better gift for you. I can give you Jesus Christ. In the name of Jesus Christ, get up and walk!" Peter took the man's right hand and helped him get up.

At once, the man's feet and ankles became strong, and he jumped up and started walking. The man went into the Temple with Peter and John. Everyone who saw the man was amazed!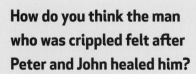

How do you think the man who was crippled felt after Peter and John healed him?

Believers Share
Acts 4:32-37

The community of people who believed in Jesus was of one heart and mind. The community shared everything. No one said, "This is mine!" They shared everything they owned. The apostles continued to teach about Jesus and shared God's love with others.

The community of believers did not have anyone who needed anything. People who had houses or fields sold them and donated that money to the community. The money was used to care for everyone so no one was in need. Barnabas was one of the people who owned a field. He sold it and gave the money to the apostles to share with others.

The believers shared everything! What can you share?

Choosing the Seven
Acts 6:1-7

The early church grew and grew. The new Christians loved God. But the number of people who were choosing to become Christians was growing so fast that the disciples couldn't keep up.

The disciples held a meeting. "It is our job to tell people about Jesus," said the disciples. "We can't feed the widows and the poor, and still have time to teach about Jesus. We need help. Select seven believers who are wise and good. These seven people will feed the widows and help the poor."

The other believers were happy the disciples chose to find some help.

Have you ever been chosen for a special job? How did that make you feel?

"We would like to choose these seven believers: Stephen, Philip, Prochorus, Nicanor, Timon, Parmenas, and Nicolaus," said the community.

The disciples said a prayer for the seven chosen and sent them to serve others.

Philip and the Ethiopian
Acts 8:26-40

Philip fed the hungry, taught others about Jesus, and helped people who were sick. While Philip was in Samaria, an angel of God talked to Philip: "Take the desert road from here. As you go, share God's love with the people you meet." So Philip set out along the desert road.

As Philip walked along the road, a carriage drove past. There was an Ethiopian man in the carriage reading a scroll about God's people.

The Ethiopian man looked very confused by what he was reading, so Philip asked the man, "Do you understand what you are reading?"

The Ethiopian man looked at Philip. "Without some help, how could I?"

The Ethiopian man invited Philip into his carriage. Philip knew what the scroll was about—Jesus! "This scroll is about Jesus. Jesus taught us how to love God and each other." The Ethiopian man believed everything Philip taught him.

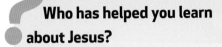

Who has helped you learn about Jesus?

While they traveled down the road, they passed by some water. "Let me be baptized!" said the Ethiopian man. They stopped the carriage, went down to the water, and Philip baptized the Ethiopian man.

Paul Changes
Acts 9:1-19

Paul and his friends were on their way to a city called Damascus. Paul had heard that there were many followers in Damascus. Paul was going to arrest Jesus' followers and bring them back to Jerusalem.

Suddenly, a bright light from heaven flashed around Paul! Paul fell to the ground and covered his eyes.

"Paul, Paul," said a voice from the light. "Why are you being unkind to my followers?" The voice was Jesus! "Get up, Paul, and go into the city," said Jesus. "Someone will come and help you." When Paul stood up, he couldn't see! Paul's friends had to lead Paul into the city.

A man named Ananias lived in the city. He was a follower of Jesus. One day Ananias heard the voice of Jesus.

"Find the man named Paul," said Jesus.

"But Paul is unkind to followers of Jesus," said Ananias. "I am afraid."

"I have chosen Paul to tell others about me," said Jesus. "You must go to him."

So even though he was afraid, Ananias went to find Paul. Paul was just sitting in a house. He still could not see.

"Paul," said Ananias, "Jesus sent me to help you." Then Ananias touched Paul's face. Immediately, Paul was able to see again!

Paul was baptized and became a follower of Jesus. Paul began to tell everyone he met about Jesus. Paul had changed.

Jesus' love changes us! How do you think Paul felt when he was changed by Jesus?

Paul Escapes
Acts 9:20-25

Paul wanted to tell everyone about Jesus, but some people did not believe he had really changed. They thought Paul was trying to trick them.

"Aren't you the same Paul who wanted to put all the followers of Jesus in jail?" asked the people who did not trust Paul.

Some of these people got so mad at Paul that they wanted to hurt him. They came up with a plan to catch Paul when he left the city. The city had a tall wall that went all the way around the city. The only way out of the city was through the gate. They had guards watching the gates of the city day and night.

Have you ever been helped by a friend? What happened?

It was time for Paul to go back home, but there was not a safe way for him to leave.

Then some of Paul's friends had an idea. They put Paul in a large basket and tied a rope to it. Then they lowered him slowly down from a window in the city wall.

Paul made it safely out of the city with the help of his friends.

The Church Grows
Acts 9:26-31

Paul arrived in Jerusalem, his home. He tried to join the disciples, Jesus' friends, but they were afraid of him. The disciples did not believe Paul had really become a follower of Jesus.

Barnabas knew that Paul loved Jesus, so he brought Paul to the disciples. Barnabas told the believers Paul's story.

Barnabas told the believers that Paul could be trusted. After this, Paul was able to work with the disciples to tell others about Jesus.

Because Paul, the disciples, and all of the followers of Jesus told everyone about Jesus' life and love, the church grew!

How do you think Paul felt when Barnabas stood up for him? Have you ever stood up for someone else?

Peter and Tabitha
Acts 9:36-43

There was a disciple named Tabitha who lived in a town called Joppa. Tabitha was a wonderful person who lived a life of good works. She loved and cared for everyone who was in need. She also made tunics and clothing for people.

Tabitha became ill. She didn't get better, and she died. Her friends washed her body and laid her body on a bed. Her friends were very sad. They heard that Peter was nearby, so they sent two people to find him.

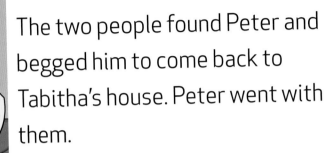

The two people found Peter and begged him to come back to Tabitha's house. Peter went with them.

Peter entered Tabitha's room. All of Tabitha's friends were there crying.

Peter asked everyone to leave Tabitha's room. He knelt down and prayed. Then Peter said, "Tabitha, get up!" Tabitha opened her eyes and sat up. Peter helped her stand as they called all of Tabitha's friends back into the room. She was alive!

How do you think Tabitha's friends felt in this story?

Peter and Cornelius
Acts 10:1-28

There was a man named Cornelius. Cornelius and his family worshipped God. Cornelius was a good man, and he and his family gave to people who needed help.

One day an angel visited Cornelius. Cornelius was surprised and scared. Cornelius asked the angel why he was there. The angel said, "Cornelius, send someone to the town of Joppa to get a man named Peter to come and visit you."

Cornelius did what the angel said. Cornelius sent two servants and a soldier to get Peter.

The next day in the town of Joppa, Peter

was sleeping when he had a dream. Peter saw a big sheet being lowered down from heaven. On the sheet were all kinds of animals that Peter was not supposed to eat. There were four-legged animals, snakes, and wild birds. A voice said to Peter, "Peter, get up. You can have all these animals to eat."

Peter said, "No, Lord! You know it is unlawful to eat all those animals. They are unclean! I do not eat those animals!"

A voice said to Peter, "Do not think of anything that God makes as unclean."

This dream happened three times. Finally, the sheet was pulled back into heaven.

Peter did not understand his dream. Just then, the messengers from Cornelius arrived.

The men said, "Cornelius has sent us. Cornelius wants you to come to his house and talk to the people there about God."

480

Peter and the messengers walked
back to Cornelius's house the next day.
When they arrived at Cornelius's house,
Cornelius was so glad to see Peter that
he fell down at Peter's feet. Peter
said, "Get up, Cornelius. I am
no better than you. I am
a man, just like you
are a man. God told
me in a dream that
every person and
every animal that
God makes
is good. All
people are
God's creations."

How do you think Cornelius felt in the story? How do you think Peter felt?

First Called Christians
Acts 11:19-30

There was trouble for the first people who believed in Jesus. They were not liked. Even though there was trouble for the first believers, the good news about Jesus could not be stopped! Soon, many people everywhere believed in Jesus!

ANTIOCH
Home of the Spice Trade
that's a spicy meatball

A lot of believers in Jesus lived in Jerusalem. Those believers sent a man named Barnabas to a town called Antioch to preach and to help the believers there. When Barnabas arrived in Antioch, he was very happy because so many people believed in Jesus!

Barnabas decided that he needed help in Antioch, so he went to get his friend, Paul. Paul joined Barnabas and the other believers in Antioch.

It was in the town of Antioch that the first believers of Jesus were called Christians.

What do you think it means to be a Christian?

Peter in Prison

Acts 12:1-17

King Herod was a mean king who never did a good thing. He made life very hard for all of Jesus' friends. King Herod put Peter in jail for telling people about Jesus.

King Herod ordered his soldiers to guard Peter so Peter would not escape. While Peter was in jail, the other Christians prayed for him.

One night Peter was sleeping in the jail. There were two chains holding Peter's arms down.

Suddenly, an angel of the Lord appeared. The angel poked Peter in his side and said, "Quick! Get up!" The chains fell off Peter's hands. The angel said, "Get dressed quickly and put on your sandals." Peter did what the angel told him to do.

When Peter was finished dressing, the angel said, "Follow me!" Peter followed the angel past the soldiers and out to the city gate. All of a sudden, the heavy gate opened by itself! Peter and the angel were walking along a street when the angel disappeared!

HEROD'S PRISON
-Come Back Soon-

Peter went to his friend Mary's house. Peter knocked on the door. A servant girl named Rhoda came to the door and said, "Who is it?" Peter said, "It is Peter." Rhoda became so excited that she ran back and told everyone that Peter was at the door.

The people in the house did not believe Rhoda. They said, "You must be wrong. We have just been praying for Peter."

7

488

Peter kept on knocking, and finally, someone opened the door for him. Everyone was amazed to see Peter!

Peter told everyone to keep quiet. Peter told his friends how God's angel had helped him escape. Then Peter said, "Tell James what has happened."

Peter turned around, left, and went to another town to tell others about Jesus.

Everyone was surprised to see Peter. Have you ever been surprised?

Timothy Is Chosen
Acts 16:1-5

Paul loved Jesus and spent a lot of time teaching others about Jesus. There was a group of Christians in the city of Lystra that Paul taught. Paul met a young boy there named Timothy. Timothy traveled with Paul and taught others about God's love. Paul sent Timothy to teach the people in Ephesus about God.

? How can you teach others about God's love?

Lydia
Acts 16:11-15

Lydia sold purple cloth. Lydia's cloth was very special, and it cost a lot of money. Only the very rich could buy Lydia's cloth.

Lydia believed in God. Sometimes Lydia and her friends went to the riverbank together. The women sat by the river and prayed to God.

One day Paul went to the riverbank and saw Lydia and her friends praying. Paul told the women about Jesus. Lydia believed what Paul told her about Jesus, and she became a follower of Jesus.

Lydia told her family about Jesus. Everyone in her family became a follower of Jesus. Lydia invited Paul to her home. Lydia helped Paul tell others about Jesus.

What would you tell others about Jesus?

Paul and Silas
Acts 16:16-40

Paul and Silas went through the town telling everyone they knew about Jesus. Some people listened to Paul and Silas. They liked what Paul and Silas had to say.

But some people did not want Paul and Silas to tell others about Jesus. They said, "Send them to jail!

So Paul and Silas were put in jail. Their hands and feet were chained to the wall. But Paul and Silas were not sad. They prayed and sang songs to God.

Suddenly, the jail began to shake! It was an earthquake! The chains on Paul and Silas fell apart. The jail door swung open.

"Oh, no!" said the jailer when he saw the open door. "I'm sure all my prisoners ran away. I'll get in trouble for letting them go."

"Don't worry," said Paul. "Everyone is still here."

Then Paul and Silas told the jailer about Jesus.

"I want to know more," said the jailer. "Come home with me and tell my whole family about Jesus."

So Paul and Silas went home with the jailer and told his whole family about Jesus. The jailer and his family became followers of Jesus.

What do you think is the most important part of this story?

Shipwrecked
Acts 27:1-44

Paul was on a ship sailing to the city of Rome. Paul was in trouble for telling people about Jesus. Paul was going to be put in jail!

The wind was blowing hard, and it tossed the ship around on the wavy sea. Paul told the captain of the ship not to sail the boat because the ship would break, and many people would die; but the ship's captain sailed the ship anyway. The ship sailed on, but the wind blew harder. The sailors tied ropes around the ship to hold it together.

The storm was so bad that the sailors threw the cargo overboard. For several days, the sailors and Paul could not see the sun or the stars because the rain came down so hard. It was scary!

Paul spoke to everyone on the ship. Paul said, "Listen! Last night in a dream, God told me that God would save everyone on this ship, but first we will be shipwrecked on an island! Now eat because you will need your strength for swimming!"

The next morning, the ship got stuck in the sand. The sailors saw an island. The captain said, "Everyone, swim to the island and save your lives!" The people who could not swim held onto planks of wood until they floated to the island. Everyone made it safely to the island. God saved Paul and everyone on the ship!

How do you think Paul felt?

1 Corinthians

First Corinthians was a letter that the apostle Paul wrote to the believers in Corinth. The believers there were arguing about the right ways to live, and had asked Paul to help them. Paul wrote them back, teaching them that loving God and each other is the most important thing.

Tips for Adults

Paul started a church in Corinth and stayed with that community of believers for a year-and-a-half. After Paul left, the Christians began to fight. They argued about who was the most important. They argued about the right way to worship God. Paul wrote this letter to correct his friends. He taught them how people can grow spiritually, learning to love and help each other.

We Are One Body
1 Corinthians 12:12-31

The believers in Corinth had many questions for Paul. The believers wanted to know how they each fit into the church.

"I am really good at playing music. Can my gift and talent be used by the church?" asked a believer.

What special things can you do?

"I am really good at praying for others," said another believer.

"I am really good at speaking in front of large crowds," said another believer.

"I am really good at listening," said another believer.

They wrote a letter to Paul for help.

"All of these gifts are very important. Each of you has been given a special gift from God. Nobody's gift is better than anyone else's. When we use our gifts together, we are like a body. We all need each other, just like we all need our body parts. We couldn't do all of the important things we need to do without our body parts, just like we can't do all the things Jesus wants us to do if we don't work together," wrote Paul.

Love
1 Corinthians 13:1-13

Paul continued teaching the people in Corinth through his letter.

He wrote, "If I don't have love, I'm like a clanging gong or a clashing cymbal.

"If I know everything but I don't have love, I'm nothing.

"If I give away everything that I have but I don't have love, it doesn't make any difference.

"Love is patient. Love is kind. Love isn't jealous. Love doesn't brag. Love isn't rude. Love isn't grumpy. Love is happy with the truth. Love never fails.

"Now faith, hope, and love remain—these three things. The greatest of these is love."

Why do you think love is the greatest thing?

Prayers & Songs

Prayer is talking to God. Praying can be silent, quiet, or loud. Prayer can be done through anything—singing, dancing, walking, or even playing. You can pray for yourself and for other people.

Tips for
Adults

The following pages are filled with songs and prayers. Invite the children to sing and pray along with you. The rhythms, music, words, and meaning will stick with your children for their whole lives.

How God Wants Us to Live

I'm a Little Helper
(Tune: I'm a Little Teapot)

I'm a little helper.
Yes, I am.

I can use my legs,
and I can use my hands.

When I get all worked up,
hear me shout.

Just ask me nicely,
and I'll help you out.

Christians Share
(Tune: Hot Cross Buns)

Christians share,
Christians share—
meet together, pray together,
and they share.

Tell of God

(Tune: Twinkle, Twinkle, Little Star)

Tell of God to all your friends.
Tell them God's love never ends.
God is good, and God is great.
Clap your hands and celebrate.
Tell of God to all your friends.
Tell them God's love never ends.

We Will Serve the Lord

(Tune: The Farmer in the Dell)

We will serve the Lord.
We will serve the Lord.
As for me and my household,
we will serve the Lord.

The Golden Rule
(Tune: My Bonnie Lies Over the Ocean)

God wants us to treat other people
as we want that they should treat us.
God wants us to treat other people
as we want that they should treat us.
Be kind, be kind.
Be kind and loving to everyone.
Be kind, be kind.
Be kind and loving to all.

Jesus Sent Them Two by Two
(Tune: Twinkle, Twinkle, Little Star)

Go to people everywhere,
tell them of my love and care.
Listen to these words I say,
I am with you every day.
Go to people everywhere,
tell them of my love and care.

Nativity Songs

Sleep, Baby Jesus
(Tune: Rock-a-Bye, Baby)

Sleep, baby Jesus,
sleep on the hay.
Mary is singing.
Little lambs play.
Joseph is watching
stars shine so bright.
So sleep, baby Jesus,
sleep through the night.

A Child Has Been Born for Us
(Tune: Mary Had a Little Lamb)

A child has been born for us, born for us,
born for us.
A child has been born for us. He is the Son
of God.

Shining Star
(Tune: This Old Man)

Shining star, shining star,
shine to show us where you are.
Shine your light on little Bethlehem;
guide the path of the wise men.

Name Him Jesus
(Tune: Did You Ever See a Lassie?)

You will name the baby Jesus,
the angel told Mary.
You will name the baby Jesus,
for he is God's Son.

Easter and Blessings Songs

On This Happy Easter Day
(Tune: The Farmer in the Dell)

Oh, we remember Jesus.
Oh, we remember Jesus.
Oh, on this happy Easter Day,
oh, we remember Jesus.

Oh, Jesus is alive.
Oh, Jesus is alive.
Oh, on this happy Easter Day,
oh, Jesus is alive.

See the Rainbow
(Tune: Mary Had a Little Lamb)

See the rainbow in the sky,
in the sky, in the sky.
See the rainbow in the sky,
with colors bright and true.

God Made All the World
(Tune: This Old Man)

God made birds; God made bees;
God made monkeys in the trees—
great big whales and even tiny fleas.
God made all the world you see.

Jesus, Jesus, Hear My Prayer
(Tune: Twinkle, Twinkle, Little Star)

Jesus, Jesus, hear my prayer.
Help me love and help me share.
You are Teacher, Healer, Friend.
I know your love never ends.
Jesus, Jesus, hear my prayer.
I'm so glad that you are there.

Mealtime Prayers

We Thank You

(Tune: The Farmer in the Dell)

We thank you for our food.
We thank you for our food.
Thank you, God, for loving us.
We thank you for our food.

Thank You, God

(Tune: Row, Row, Row Your Boat)

Thank, thank, thank you, God.
Thank you for our food.
We know that you take care of us.
Now we thank you for our food.

Movement Prayer

Dear God, *(hands together at heart)*
Thank you *(jump with joy)*
for the sun, the moon, *(arms form a circle)*
and the stars; *(index fingers point up)*
for winter, *(shake as if you were cold)*
spring, *(stretch arms like you just woke up)*
summer, *(fan yourself from the heat)*
and fall; *(move hands toward the ground like falling leaves)*
for the birds in the air *(flap your arms)*
and the fish in the sea; *(make a fish face)*
for dogs and cats that keep me company;
(make whiskers with your fingers)
for friends and family that bring me joy.
(hug yourself)
All of these things bless me. *(smile)*
Help me bless everything I see. Amen.
(bring hands back together at heart)